A Brief History of Cumberland College 1825-1861

A BRIEF HISTORY OF CUMBERLAND COLLEGE 1825-1861

THE ORIGINAL CUMBERLAND PRESBYTERIAN EDUCATIONAL INSTITUTION IN PRINCETON, KENTUCKY

Matthew H. Gore

2014
Boardman Books (USA)
Bartlett, Tennessee

The Boardman Bloodhound Logo was designed by Denis McLoughlin in the late-1940s. Mr. McLoughlin (1918-2002) was the art director for the original and long defunct Boardman Books in London, England. This graphic is used with his very kind written permission.

Second Edition
Published by Boardman Books
Bartlett, Tennessee

ISBN: 978-0692373576 (0692373578)

10 9 8 7 6 5 4 3 2

*In loving memory of James W. Knight,
James Boardman, and Harry Gore
this work is respectfully dedicated*

CONTENTS

PREFACE

Cumberland College in Princeton, Kentucky, operated from 1826 to 1860. It was founded as the official college of the Cumberland Presbyterian Church but lost that designation in 1842, due primarily to the great financial difficulties that had plagued the school's existence to that point. After 1842, Green River Synod of the Cumberland Presbyterian Church replaced the Cumberland Presbyterian General Assembly as sponsoring body for Cumberland College.

I first became interested in Cumberland College and Franceway Ranna Cossitt in the 1990s while I was writing **A History of the Cumberland Presbyterian Church in Kentucky to 1988**. At that time, it occurred to me that there might be an audience for an expanded history of that long defunct Kentucky institution. Just less than a hundred persons are known to have graduated from Cumberland College although many more attended. Many of these graduates and students went on to prominence both in the Cumberland Presbyterian Church and other occupations. Their decedents, it seems, are legion.

Observant readers will notice a great deal of similarity between this work and chapter eight of my larger Kentucky history. Given that several new sources have come to light since I wrote that work I hope that this expanded text is a worthy investment for persons who already own that earlier volume.

Matthew H. Gore
Memphis, Tennessee, 2010

INTRODUCTION

In his 1899 **History of the Cumberland Presbyterian Church**, B.W. McDonnold states,

> Though this church had its origin among the pioneer settlers of Kentucky and Tennessee, far from literary and commercial centers; though its first members were hardy and simple-hearted backwoodsmen;. . . though the scholastic training of many of its first preachers did not meet the requirements of the rigid Presbyterian rule; yet its ministers and people have ever been the friends and promoters of liberal education.[1]

Despite the common nineteenth century rumor that Cumberland Presbyterians were opposed to education, the denomination sponsored a number of educational institutions.[2] The first of these was Cumberland College founded in Princeton, Kentucky, in 1825.

The enthusiasm for schools which nineteenth century Cumberland Presbyterians apparently possessed was either reflected or inspired by the General Assembly's committee on education. In 1845 this committee went so far as to recommend a widespread scheme of Cumberland Presbyterian education. The recommendation required the establishment of schools "within the bounds of every congregation" and "a presbyterial school within the bounds of every presbytery." These institutions were to feed the "University at Lebanon, and the colleges at Princeton, Beverly, and Uniontown" and "constitute a system of education worthy of the best efforts of the

---

[1] B. W. McDonnold, **History of the Cumberland Presbyterian Church** (Nashville, Tennessee, 1899), 563.

[2] Thomas H. Campbell, **Good News on the Frontier** (Memphis, Tennessee, 1965), 109.

1

church."[3]

This emphasis on education continued with apparent success from 1845 to 1851. In 1846 the General Assembly's Committee on Education reported, "Numerous congregational, Presbyterial, and Synodical Schools have been planted and are enjoying a high degree of prosperity." However, in 1851, the General Assembly felt it necessary to warn, "We suggest the necessity of much prudence and caution, lest in the eagerness to build up colleges the church squander its means, paralyze its energies, and ultimately fail of raising its institutions to the high standard desired." Despite this warning and the warnings of each assembly following, by 1860 there were, or had been, at least twenty Cumberland Presbyterian institutions of higher education calling themselves colleges or universities.[4]

---

[3]McDonnold, **History of the Cumberland Presbyterian Church**, 565-66; Campbell, **Good News**, 105.

[4]Minutes of the General Assembly of the Cumberland Presbyterian Church, May 26, 1846; McDonnold, **History of the Cumberland Presbyterian Church**, 566-67.

THE IDEA FOR A COLLEGE

Franceway Ranna Cossitt

The question of education long troubled Cumberland Presbyterian clergy. One of the key elements behind the split resulting in the founding of Cumberland Presbytery was the accusation that Cumberland ministers did not have the educational background required by the Presbyterian Church. After the formation of independent Cumberland Presbytery, the new church determined that no one would be able to say her ministers were deficient.

Logan Presbytery addressed the subject of formal ministerial education during its spring meeting of 1825. The presbytery planned that a presbyterial school be formed and formed a committee to implement the plan. This committee acted through 1825 and into the spring of 1826.[5]

The idea of establishing an educational institution for the entire Cumberland Presbyterian Church reached the floor of the general Cumberland Synod in October of 1825. Rev. Franceway Ranna Cossitt championed the idea of a Cumberland Presbyterian College through a series of letters written to prominent ministers

---

[5]Minutes of Logan Presbytery of the Cumberland Presbyterian Church, April 8, 1825, October 13, 1825, April 3-5, 1826.

before the meeting of synod and on the floor of the synod as well.[6]

Franceway Ranna Cossitt, the name actually a corruption of François René, was born at Claremont, New Hampshire, on April 24, 1790, and began his ministry in the Episcopal Church in New England. Both his father and grandfather had been the pastors of the Episcopal church in Claremont. After graduating from Vermont's Middlebury College, he taught for two years at Morristown in New Jersey before being employed to administer Vine Hill Academy on North Carolina's Roanoak River.[7]

According to Richard Beard, writing shortly after Cossitt's death, Franceway Cossitt originally intended to become a lawyer. However, after a personal conversion experience, he turned to the ministry. He studied theology at New Haven, Connecticut, in a school that was eventually merged into The General Theological Seminary of the Episcopal Church in New York City. Anglican Bishop Thomas Church Brownell, of the Diocese of Connecticut, licensed Cossitt as a "lay reader" in about late-1819 or early-1820.[8]

At the urging of wealthy North Carolina emigres, Cossitt settled in Tennessee and established himself as a teacher in a now extinct community named New York on the Cumberland River near Clarksville. The date of Cossitt's westward migration is not known, but he was in Tennessee by 1821. In the fall, after a camp meeting on

---

[6]Richard Beard, "Brief Historical Sketch of Cumberland College, At Princeton, Kentucky. 1825-1861," **Theological Medium, A Cumberland Presbyterian Quarterly**, 12 (April, 1876), 130; Cumberland Synod of the Cumberland Presbyterian Church (Franceway Ranna Cossitt), **A Brief View of Cumberland College, Founded by the Synod of the Cumberland Presbyterian Church, Near Princeton, Kentucky. By a Committee of Synod 1828** (Washington, D.C., 1829), 3; Thomas H. Campbell, **Studies in Cumberland Presbyterian History** (Nashville, Tennessee, 1944), 228-29.

[7]G. Frank Burns, **Phoenix Rising; the Sesquicentenial History of Cumberland University, 1842-1992** (Lebanon, Tennessee, 1992), 19; Richard Beard, "Franceway Ranna Cossitt, D.D. 1822-1863," **Brief Biographical Sketches of Some of the Early Ministers of the Cumberland Presbyterian Church** (Nashville, Tennessee, 1867), 154-57.

[8]Beard, "Franceway Ranna Cossitt," 154-57; "Thomas Church Brownell," retreived February 11, 2007, from http://famousamericans.net/.

Wells Creek in Stewart County, attached himself to the Cumberland Presbyterian Denomination. Even after his ordination in 1822 by Anderson Presbytery, Cossitt continued to teach. On February 19, 1822, he married Lucinda Blair of Montgomery County, Tennessee, whom Richard Beard calls "a lady of unusual personal attractions."[9]

On the frontier there was little opportunity to advance in the field of education. Further, Cossitt's plans to publish a newspaper titled the **Western Star** collapsed. In about 1823 or 1824, Franceway and Lucinda settled in Elkton in Todd County, Kentucky, establishing a school there. It is likely that the Cossitts' first daughter, Anne Catherine, was born in Elkton on October 11, 1824. Cossitt's academic ambitions led him to involve two or three lawyers in his plans. Elkton's John Grey and Russellville's Ephraim M. Ewing were certainly involved and a second lawyer from Elkton was mentioned but not named by Cossitt. On the floor of Cumberland Synod, Cossitt's proposal found vocal support from Finis Ewing, Samuel King, Robert Donnell, David Lowry, John Barnett, and William Barnett. Ewing, "while he warned against pride, self-confidence and trusting in an arm of flesh, actually made the most lucid and powerful argument in favor of ministerial education."[10]

After debate, prominent support lead to the following declaration entered into the minutes of October 22, 1825,

> Whereas, the Synod of the Cumberland Presbyterian Church have long considered literature a most excellent auxiliary in promoting the interest of our holy religion, and fearing that the ordinary system of education pursued in most of our public institutions has too great a tendency to unfit the pupil for the common employment

---

[9]Burns, **Phoenix Rising**, 19; Beard, "Franceway Ranna Cossitt," 154-57.

[10]Beard, "Franceway Ranna Cossitt", 157; Beard, "Brief Historical Sketch,", 130-131; "Cossitt Family Information," retreived from http://www.cumberland.org/ hfcpc/minister/Cossitt.htm; F. R. Cossitt, **The Life and Times of Rev. Finis Ewing One of the Fathers and Founders of the Cumberland Presbyterian Church, to Which is Added Remarks on Davidson's History , or, a Review of His Chapters on the Revival of 1800, and His History of the Cumberland Presbyterians** (Louisville, Kentucky, 1853), 281.

of life, to unnerve bodily vigor, and consequently to produce mental imbecility; and considering active exercise essentially necessary to bodily health, and consequently to mental energy, without which the great object of education is defeated; they, for the advantage of the rising generation in general, and their own candidates and children in particular, have thought proper to adopt the following resolutions:

Resolved, That this Synod establish a college, to be known as the Cumberland Presbyterian College, in some central situation within her bounds; that the highest judicature shall in the future constitute a board of trustees, but for the present five commissioners shall be chosen, any three of whom may act to select a site, receive donations and subscriptions, purchase land, and make the necessary arrangements for bring the institution into operation, and shall have power to appoint a committee of five, either in or out of their body, to act as a board of trustees until the next meeting of the highest judicature. In the selection of a site, the commissioners shall have regard to donations, healthfulness, and other conveniences of the place, and shall have power to purchase a tract of not less than two hundred nor more than five hundred acres of land for the benefit of the institution.

That the internal government of the seminary shall be under a president and such professors and tutors as the trustees shall please to appoint, who shall hold their offices during good behavior or the pleasure of the trustees.

That annexed to the institution, there shall be a theological department, under the care of the professors of divinity, whose duty it shall be to teach biblical criticism, ecclesiastical history, etc., and to deliver lectures twice a week during the winter session. Until such time as the funds will justify the employment of stated professors at the institution, the board of trustees shall appoint men to write a certain number of lectures on subjects assigned them (all which shall compose a body of divinity), whose duty it shall be to forward their lectures to whomsoever the trustees may appoint to deliver them to the students and examine them thereon.

That the committee acting as a board of trustees shall appoint a skillful manager to superintend the farming establishment, to erect cabins and other buildings, and to take charge of the boarding establishment.

That every student shall be employed in manual labor not less than two nor more than three hours every day, and for this purpose the whole number of students shall be divided into suitable

6

classes. The superintendent of the farm shall call on each class in rotation to perform their term of daily labor, and shall be privileged to employ them at such kind of labor, principally agricultural, as may afford them useful exercise, and conduce to the interests of the institution.

That so much of the produce of the farm as may be necessary, shall be appropriated to the boarding establishment.

That it shall be the duty of the faculty to forbid the use of feather beds, and to restrict the students to a frugal and wholesome diet, avoiding all luxuries.

That the rate of tuition shall be thirty dollars per year, and that there shall be no charge for boarding and washing, unless the necessities of the institution may require it; but in no event shall this charge exceed the sum of thirty dollars per year.

That the privileges of the institution extend to all young gentlemen of good moral character who will comply with the terms of tuition.

That all students shall pay semi-annually in advance the sums required by the rules of the institution.

That all money collected after paying the salaries of the officers of the institution, shall pass into the treasury and go to constitute a permanent fund for future exigencies, but be under the control of the board of trustees, who shall have liberty to appoint their treasurer and librarian.

That the board of trustees, or commissioners appointed as such, shall have power to appoint a certain number of agents to solicit donations, whose duty it shall be to report to the board and pay over all money received.

That persons appointed to receive donations shall be authorized to receive money, books, horses, stock, or farming utensils.

That as funds increase, the board shall have the power to make arrangements for the establishment of professorships and scholarships, each of which, if founded by a society or individual, shall be named for or by that society or individual.

That a collegiate course, entitling a student to a diploma, shall consist of four years' regular study, and the following branches shall be taught during the first year: English and Latin grammar, *Corderii, Selectœ e Profanis*, Virgil, and Blair's Lectures, abridged. During the second year, Horace, Cicero, Sallust, Greek Grammar, Greek Testament, and Grœca Minora. During the third and forth years, the following sciences: Geography, Rhetoric,

Logic, Mathematics, Natural and Moral Philosophy, Astronomy, and History, with other such sciences as the faculty may direct.

That Candidates for the ministry in the Cumberland Presbyterian Church shall not be received in the institution unless they produce satisfactory testimonials from their Presbyteries, and shall not be entitled to a diploma until they are adjudged thoroughly acquainted with the sciences required by the Discipline of the Cumberland Presbyterian Church.

That all students shall have the privilege, but none shall be required, to attend the lectures on theology, except the candidates for the ministry in the Cumberland Presbyterian Church.

That, if deemed expedient, the board of trustees shall have power to make necessary arrangements for establishing a printing office to publish a periodical paper, books, tracts, etc., and all profits arising therefrom shall belong to the permanent fund.

That the Rev. John Barnett, of Caldwell county, Kentucky, Rev. Franceway R. Cossitt, of Elkton, Kentucky, Gen. Joseph M. Street, of Shawneetown, Illinois, Ephraim M. Ewing, Esq., of Russellville, Kentucky, and Joseph D. Hamilton, Esq., of Logan county, Kentucky, be commissioners to carry the above resolution into effect.

Wm. Barnett, Moderator.

Hiram McDaniel, Clerk.
Princeton, Kentucky, Oct. 21, 1825.[11]

This resolution provided a comprehensive plan for the establishment and operation of an educational institution. It proposed to establish a "manual labor school" to be known as Cumberland Presbyterian College at a central point within the area of the denomination. In the early-1800s, an agricultural manual labor system of education developed by Philipp Emanuel Von Fellenberg of Hofwyl, Switzerland, was in vogue in the United States. Overall, the concept was to establish a school that could combine labor and study in order to provide a healthy and inexpensive means of training potential Cumberland Presbyterian ministers. It was a project for which the synod all but demanded the financial support of the denomination stating, "each ordained minister of said Church shall

---

[11]Minutes of Cumberland Synod of the Cumberland Presbyterian Church, October 22, 1825.

use his best exertions to obtain donations for the benefit of said institution," and appointing "agents to receive cash or property" in each presbytery.[12]

---

[12]Minutes of the Cumberland Synod of the Cumberland Presbyterian Church, October 22, 1825; Beard, "Brief Historical Sketch," 131; Cossitt, **A Brief View of Cumberland College**, 3; Campbell, **Studies in Cumberland Presbyterian History**, 229; Henry Bascom Evans, "History of the Organization and Administration of Cumberland Presbyterian Colleges" (Ph.D. dissertation, George Peabody College for Teachers, 1938), 71.

THE VICINITY OF A LARGE TOWN

In 1825, Southwestern Kentucky was understood to be the central area of the Cumberland Presbyterian Church. The commission appointed was to study that area and select a site for the proposed college. This commission, empowered by the synod with the authority to establish a school and initiate its operation, met for the first time on October 24, 1825.[13]

> The Synod of the Cumberland Presbyterian Church, at its last meeting, held at Princeton, Kentucky, on the 21st day of October, 1825, having entered into a resolution, and adopted a constitution for the establishment of a college in some situation within its bounds, and having proceeded to appoint Rev. John Barnett, Rev. F. R. Cossitt, E. M. Ewing, Esq., J. D. Hamilton, Esq., and Joseph M. Street, commissioners, to determine upon the proper location of said college, and for other purposes, and the said commissioners having met on the 24th day of October, 1825, appointed to meet again at Princeton, Kentucky, on the first Monday in January, 1826, to proceed to the performance of the duties assigned to them by the Synod, and adjourned.[14]

Several factors influenced the committee appointed to select a site for the college. "The College should not be situated in the vicinity of a large town" because of the temptations to "extravagance, vice and dissipation" present in "commercial places." Further,

> The College should be located at a place which enjoys pure air, good water, and a fertile soil, so near to some small village, that the faculty and students may enjoy the convenience of a post office, and furnish themselves with books, stationery, clothes, &c.

Toward this end, the synod had four specific Kentucky sites in mind

---

[13]Beard, "Brief Historical Sketch," 131-32.

[14]**Ibid.**, 132.

for the location of the Cumberland Presbyterian College: Princeton in Caldwell County, Hopkinsville in Christian County, Elkton in Todd County, and Russellville in Logan County. The decision of which of these communities would host the proposed institution was to be at least partially decided by the cash amount each would be willing to contribute in order to have the college located there. Cumberland synod dictated that the commission charged with establishing a college meet in early January in each of these towns in order to judge them.[15]

> In compliance with the order of Synod, and their own agreement, Rev. John Barnett, Rev. F. R. Cossitt, E. M. Ewing, Esq., Joseph D. Hamilton, Esq., and Joseph M. Street, met at the house of Mr. Mitchausan, in the town of Princeton, Kentucky on the first Monday in January, 1826, it being the second day of the month, when Rev. John Barnett was called to the chair, and Joseph M. Street was appointed Secretary.[16]

This meeting in Princeton was followed by another in Hopkinsville, a third in Elkton, and still a fourth in Russellville. Each town was assessed for a site and for the amount that might be donated or subscribed if the college were located there. On January 13, 1826, thanks to outstanding pledges of monetary support which were reported to amount to between $15,000 and $28,000 in cash and property from the residents, the commission decided in favor of Princeton, "a healthy and pleasant village," in Caldwell County.[17]

The site selected was located about a mile from "the little rural village of Princeton" on a farm owned by Mercer Wadlington. The farm was between 400 and 500 acres with an "unfailing" spring and had, in the opinion of the commission, "good improvements" or

---

[15]Cossitt, **A Brief View of Cumberland College**, 4; Minutes of Cumberland Synod of the Cumberland Presbyterian Church, October 22, 1825.

[16]Beard, "Brief Historical Sketch," 132.

[17]**Ibid.**, 132-34; Campbell, **Studies in Cumberland Presbyterian History**, 232; Evans, "Cumberland Presbyterian Colleges," 73; "Cumberland College," **Banner of Peace and Cumberland Presbyterian Advocate** (November 24, 1843), 2.

11

buildings. They agreed to pay Wadlington $6,000 for the property and were to take possession on March 1, 1826. The commission also arranged that the trustees of the college would have the authority to purchase an additional 73 acres in the same proximity.[18]

Also, at the meeting of the commission on January 13, 1826, it was,

> further ordered that the Rev. F. R. Cossitt be, and is hereby, chosen teacher of said institution, and that he be allowed at the rate of one thousand dollars in commonwealth paper per annum for his services, to be paid semi-annually, in advance, from the time of his entering into the institution. That the Rev. John Barnett be appointed manager of the farm and boarding establishment. That the Rev. John Barnett, Rev. David Lowry, John H. Phelps, Asbury Harpending, and John Mercer, Esq., be, and they are hereby, appointed a committee to act as a Board of Trustees, and that all the aforesaid appointments continue until the next meeting of the Synod; and, furthermore, that the said trustees take into their possession the subscriptions and donations, receive titles for the lands donated in the name of the trustees for the use of said college; collect the funds as they may become due, and do all acts and things that they may deem necessary to bring the said institution into full and complete operation.[19]

With this meeting, the authority of the commission ended to be replaced by that of the Board of Trustees of Cumberland Presbyterian College. The first meeting of the trustees took place on January 20, 1826, on the farm they intended to purchase. Present were John Barnett, David Lowry, Asbury Harpending, John Mercer, and John H. Phelps. John Barnett was elected chairman and John H. Phelps, clerk.[20]

At this first meeting the purchase of Mercer Wadlington's

---

[18]Cossitt, **A Brief View of Cumberland College**, 4; Beard, "Brief Historical Sketch of Cumberland College," 133.

[19]Beard, "Brief Historical Sketch of Cumberland College," 133.

[20]**Ibid.**, 133-34.

farm concluded. The price agreed upon was $6,000 with $1,500 to be paid in advance. The remainder, $4,500, was to be paid in two payments of $2,250 each at the conclusion of one and two years. Without funds to make the initial payment, the trustees were forced to borrow the money. But, in light of the pledges made by the public in the area of Princeton, this could not have been foreseen as a problem by the trustees. When, in turn, the two remaining payments came due and still no significant amount had been collected from those who had pledged it, the trustees had to borrow the funds to meet each.[21]

At the second meeting of the trustees, on April 24, 1826, the following was recorded,

> *Resolved,* Unanimously, by this Board, that they will encumber by mortgage, the lands conveyed to the trustees of the Cumberland Presbyterian College by Mercer Wadlington and his wife, to the securities in the bonds given by the trustees of said institution to said Wadlington, for the purchase money of said lands.

Also, at this meeting, Asbury Harpending, the board's treasurer resigned only to be elected again and bonded for $20,000.[22]

At the board meeting of January 2, 1827, a resolution passed allowing David Lowry to attempt collection of the pledges made in support of the college. Lowry had the choice of making his collections "verbally or by letter." However, he was to use "a mild and persuasive manner."[23]

During the history of the college when it received support from Cumberland Synod and, later, the General Assembly of the Cumberland Presbyterian Church, it was common for the trustees to appoint fund raising agents to solicit funds. Among these agents were many of the church's prominent ministers. Some of them include Reuben Burrow and A. G. Gibson who traveled through East Tennessee and North Carolina in 1826 but failed to even pay their

---

[21]**Ibid.**, 134-35.

[22]**Ibid.**, 136.

[23]**Ibid.**, 137.

own expenses, Laban Jones who was commissioned to travel the entire United States from late-1827 to late-1828 but only collected $143.25, Cyrus W. Wilson, Laban Jones, Robert Rennick, Caleb Weeden, Matthew H. Bone, Samuel M. Cowan, William Devault and Henry F. Delany—all appointed in 1828, John W. Ogden and Matthew H. Bone who turned over $78.47 on November 21, 1829, and Hiram McDaniel, John L. Dillard, and William Bigham who apparently did not cover their expenses.[24]

Finis Ewing, certainly one of the most prominent Cumberland Presbyterian ministers, was regarded as one of the "warmest friends and most liberal patrons" of the Cumberland Presbyterian College. In a letter to William Harris, Ewing indicated that he wished the profits from the publication of his lectures to go to the college. However, Finis Ewing's generosity to higher education was not often emulated by his colleagues.[25]

---

[24]**Ibid.**, 140-41; Minutes of Cumberland Synod of the Cumberland Presbyterian Church, October 24, 1828.

[25]Cossitt, **Life and Times of Rev. Finis Ewing**, 281-82.

CUMBERLAND COLLEGE

Tradition has it that Franceway Cossitt began his employment on March 1, 1826. As the only employee retained by the college at the time this date must mark the beginning of the Cumberland Presbyterian College as an institution. Conditions on the site in 1826 were primitive for the six students enrolled. The Wadlington farmhouse served as a boarding house for students and a brick structure of six rooms was also erected as a dormitory. Each room was intended to house four students. Log cabins were erected for the remainder of the college housing needs. The main building of Cumberland Presbyterian College was also constructed of logs. It was two stories high and had stone chimneys. By the end of 1826, there were about 60 students in the Cumberland Presbyterian College.[26]

John Barnett, the college's second employee, was to manage the farm and boarding facilities. Cumberland Synod left the matter of his wages vague. "A reasonable compensation" was prescribed. Barnett could require at least two hours a day of manual labor from each of the college students. He was also allowed to bring his own property to the farm and collect compensation for the use of it.[27]

With Cossitt in place as "teacher" or president and Barnett as manager of the farm and boarding, it was necessary to recruit additional faculty. On June 28, 1826, the board,

> *Resolved,* That in employing a teacher, or assistant teacher, in the said college, due regard shall always be paid to qualification, and unless candidates for office produce a diploma, they must undergo

---

[26]Cossitt, **A Brief View of Cumberland College**, 5; J. M. Howard and J. M. Hubbert, "The Cumberland Presbyterian Church," **Presbyterians: A Popular Narrative of their Origin, Progress, Doctrines, and Achievements** (New York, 1892), 473; Beard, "Brief Historical Sketch of Cumberland College," 135-36; Beard, "Franceway Ranna Cossitt," 158.

[27]Minutes of Cumberland Synod of the Cumberland Presbyterian Church, October 22, 1825; Beard, "Brief Historical Sketch of Cumberland College," 136.

an examination on the branches they profess to teach, by the faculty of the college, in the presence of the trustees.[28]

On September 18, 1826, the Board of Trustees employed Daniel L. Morrison, later known to the students as Judge Morrison, as an assistant teacher. Morrison's compensation was to be $550 per year paid semi-annually.[29]

The faculty and farm manager were to be in full control of the day to day operation of the college as is evidenced by this directive of the trustees made on March 27, 1826,

> That the faculty direct what kind of diet is thought to be wholesome and frugal, according to the custom of other colleges, and that they shall give any other directions which they may think proper in relation to the boarding, lodging, and cooking establishments.[30]

A committee, under the nominal leadership of Henry F. Delany, was instructed by Cumberland Synod to approach Kentucky's legislative General Assembly, meeting in Frankfort, and request a charter for Cumberland Presbyterian College. The legislature showed hesitation only over the name of the institution fearing the inclusion of "Presbyterian" might prompt resentment from other denominations. Given this, a charter was requested for Cumberland College and granted on January 8, 1827, however, Richard Beard noted that this name change "created some dissatisfaction."[31]

---

[28]Minutes of the Board of Trustees of Cumberland Presbyterian College, June 28, 1826, as recorded in Richard Beard's "Brief Historical Sketch of Cumberland College," 137.

[29]Beard, "Brief Historical Sketch of Cumberland College," 137, 141.

[30]Minutes of the Board of Trustees of Cumberland Presbyterian College, March 27, 1826, as recorded in Richard Beard's, "Brief Historical Sketch of Cumberland College," 136.

[31]Richard Beard, "Brief Historical Sketch of Cumberland College," 137-38; Acts of the Legislature of the Commonwealth of Kentucky, relating to Incorporating Cumberland College of Princeton, Kentucky, January 8, 1827.

This state charter intended to insure that no student be denied admission based on religion and that the Commonwealth of Kentucky made fiscal gain by the granting,

> . . .the Synod of the Cumberland Presbyterian Church in the State of Kentucky, has determined upon establishing an extensive seminary of learning, near Princeton, Caldwell county, to the support of which that body are pledged to use their undivided efforts, and from which no student is to be excluded in consequence of his religious opinions, or the religious opinions of his parents, guardians or relations; and that said seminary of learning shall be conducted upon free, liberal and enlightened principles: and whereas, the establishment of an institution of this kind, within the State of Kentucky, if conducted upon the above liberal plan, will be of great advantage to the State, by disseminating knowledge and useful learning, and by introducing into our state, students from Tennessee, Illinois, Indiana, and other States, thereby increasing our pecuniary advantages and intercourse with others. And whereas, the moderate terms presented in the constitution of said institution, for education, encourages the hope of greatly extending useful knowledge: and whereas, there are but few seminaries of learning in that part of our own or the adjoining States: Therefore,
>
> Sec. 1. Be it enacted by the General Assembly of the Commonwealth of Kentucky, That a seminary of learning is hereby established near the town of Princeton, in Caldwell county, to be known by the name of Cumberland College.[32]

The charter placed legal control of Cumberland College in the hands of "the Trustees of the Cumberland College" which it made "able and capable in law, to have, possess, purchase, receive, enjoy and retain, hold or dispose of. . . lands, tenements, rents, annuities, pensions and other hereditaments." These trustees were to meet at least twice a year. Further, the trustees "shall be capable in law to sue and be sued, plead and be impleaded, in any court. . . in this State and elsewhere." The heart of the trustees power was their stated ability to "establish fundamental ordinances, rules and by-laws" as long as they

---

[32]Acts of the Legislature of the Commonwealth of Kentucky, relating to Incorporating Cumberland College of Princeton, Kentucky, January 8, 1827.

did not contradict the laws of the Commonwealth. A President of the Board, a secretary, and a treasurer were authorized. The president was to preside at meetings, keep order, and determine the agenda.[33]

In section five of the charter an oath of office was dictated to be sworn before the Justice of the Peace of Caldwell County "or before the county court of the county in which such trustee may reside." The oath stated,

> I, (A. B.) do swear or affirm, that I will, to the best of my skill and judgement, faithfully and truly discharge the duties of a trustee of the Cumberland College, pursuant to the laws and constitution of Kentucky, and the constitution of the United States, and the charter granted by this act, without favor, affection or partiality. So help me God.[34]

By this charter of 1827, the trustees were given the power to "constitute and appoint" faculty for Cumberland College. Of course they had, on the instruction of Cumberland Synod, already undertaken this task. The charter names the faculty, "the President and Professors of the Cumberland College." Perhaps it was at this time that Franceway Cossitt began to be referred to as president rather than just *teacher* as he was in the synod's original instructions for founding the college. As to the faculty the Kentucky General Assembly prescribed,

> a President, and necessary and proper professors, tutors, masters, and assistants, for instructing the students and scholars of said College, in all the liberal arts and sciences, and in the ancient and modern tongues and languages, as they shall be nominated and appointed to teach.[35]

Section eleven of the charter dealt with one aspect of Cumberland College that never came to fruition.

---

[33] Ibid.

[34] Ibid.

[35] Ibid.

That it shall and may be lawful for the trustees of said College to establish and endow one or more professorships of theology or other professorships, to be separate and distinct from the literary department of said College; and each and every department of theology which may be established, shall at all times regulate their own affairs without interfering in any way with the by-laws or statutes of the College, or of any other department thereof; and the privilege is hereby reserved to each and every regular denomination of Christians, to establish a professorship of theology in said College, provided they furnish the funds necessary for its support.[36]

Clearly, the legislature hoped that a true theological seminary would be established in Princeton.

The last recorded meeting of the Trustees of the Cumberland Presbyterian College was held on January 2, 1827, within a week of the granting of the charter. The Trustees of Cumberland College held their first meeting on May 28, 1827. David Lowry, Henry F. Delany, A. Harpending, John H. Phelps, and Will Lander were present. The trustees proceeded to elect the officers authorized to them by charter. David Lowry was elected President, Will Lander, secretary, and A. Harpending, treasurer.[37]

Cumberland Synod, meeting on November 24, 1827, acknowledged the charter as granted by the General Assembly of the State of Kentucky, but not, however, without reservations. Besides the change in the name of the institution which has already been noted, the delegates to synod objected to that portion of the charter which reserved the power of change to that body. The synod feared that "unconditional acceptance" of the charter might "deprive the Synod of the Cumberland Presbyterian Church of its control" over Cumberland College, "and the funds, thereof."[38]

The synod passed the following resolution to insure their continued control,

---

[36]Ibid.

[37]Beard, "Brief Historical Sketch of Cumberland College,"138.

[38]Minutes of Cumberland Synod of the Cumberland Presbyterian Church, November 24, 1825.

Resolved by the Synod of the Cumberland Presbyterian Church, assembled at Russellville, That said charter is accepted, but if said Legislature should at any time hereafter repeal said charter in whole, or shall take away the powers of said Synod to appoint trustees for said institution, or shall make an alteration which shall not meet the approbation of said Synod, in that event all the funds of said institution, real, personal, or mixed, shall revert and pass to and be vested in such trustees as the Synod shall have appointed, to be subject to the future control and disposition of said Synod, or the General Assembly of said Church, should one be constituted.

A committee consisting of William Harris, Daniel L. Morrison, and E. M. Ewing was appointed to present this resolution to the legislature and ask for an amendment to the charter.[39]

Graduates of Cumberland College in 1827, were Fielding Jones and John Moore. Jones entered the legal profession and Moore became a professor at a medical college in St. Louis. In 1828, A. W. Wadlington, Henry B. King, and F. C. Usher graduated. Of these, only Usher served the Cumberland Presbyterian Church. Franceway and Lucinda Cossitt's second child, Asbury Haspending Cossitt, was also born in Princeton in 1828.[40]

Despite the frontier situation in which Cumberland College was founded and despite the often provincial reputation of the Cumberland Presbyterian Church, Cumberland College demonstrated a remarkably progressive attitude by admitting female students beginning with the first school year. The first three women admitted as students to Cumberland College, and thus to any American coeducational educational institution, were Ann Harpending in 1826 and the sisters Mary and Melinda Barnett in 1827. Oberlin College, generally regarded as the first American coeducational institution, was not founded until 1837. The Barnett girls were the daughters of faculty member John Barnett but this should in no way cheapen the

---

[39]Minutes of Cumberland Synod of the Cumberland Presbyterian Church, November 24, 1827.

[40]"Cossitt Family Information;" Beard, "Brief Historical Sketch of Cumberland College," 171.The spelling "Haspending" is retained here because it is consistent with most printed sources. More likely, however, the name was probably "Harpending" after the notable minister of that name.

accomplishment. There is no record yet discovered of these or any other women having graduated from Cumberland College.[41]

---

[41]"Treasurer's Book of Cumberland College, 1826-1848." Alphabetic typescript by Sam Steger. Princeton, Kentucky, Public Library; Matthew H. Gore, **A History of the Cumberland Presbyterian Church in Kentucky to 1988** (Memphis, Tennessee, 2000), 277. Malinda, as used in the typescript, was probably a corruption of Melinda.

THE QUESTION OF FINANCES

By the meeting of Cumberland Synod from October 21-25, 27, 1828, in Franklin, Williamson County, Tennessee, the financial concerns of Cumberland College attracted the interest of the delegates who resolved that an auditor be appointed to examine all accounts and report annually. Daniel L. Morrison was recommended for the position.[42]

Also, in 1828, the synod delegated authority over the Board of Trustees of Cumberland College to a standing commission of ministers all located in relative proximity to Princeton. These members were Franceway R. Cossitt, appointed as the commission's moderator, and in quite a curious position as his own employer, John Barnett, Hiram McDaniel, James Johnston, William T. Hutchison, Matthew H. Bone, John W. Ogden, David W. McLin, Alexander Chapman, Aaron Shelby, William Harris, and their elders. Any five members with five elders were to constitute a quorum. This commission had the power to remove trustees and appoint new ones in their place. Cossitt, an employee of the college, as moderator of this commission with the authority to direct its actions "as he may see proper" had effective control over the very trustees who were supposed to supervise him.[43]

Many of Cumberland College's students were moving along the path toward ordination in the Cumberland Presbyterian Church. In order that these candidates and licentiates could be more effectively under the care of presbytery, a new presbytery was dictated to constitute on November 29, 1828, Princeton Presbytery. This presbytery included "all that part of Caldwell county, in Kentucky, lying between the Cumberland and Tradewater rivers, and the congregation of Piny Fork." Members included Franceway R.

---

[42]Minutes of Cumberland Synod of the Cumberland Presbyterian Church, October 24, 1828.

[43]Minutes of Cumberland Synod of the Cumberland Presbyterian Church, October 24, 1828.

Cossitt, David Lowry, John W. Ogden, and James Johnston. Franceway Cossitt was appointed to be the first moderator of Princeton Presbytery and "all candidates and licentiates becoming members of College shall be under care and jurisdiction of said Princeton Presbytery."[44]

The first new faculty member added by the Trustees of Cumberland College was authorized at their meeting on May 30, 1829, "*Resolved,* That the Faculty be instructed to make known, that a teacher of French would be employed, to give instruction from the commencement of the next session. . ." Bertrand Guerin was appointed to this position. In addition to French, he was to teach Latin, English grammar, and geography. His salary was $400 per year. Unfortunately, Guerin, "a foreigner," proved to be "a literary vagabond." Due to objectionable conduct, he was called before a committee of the General Assembly in May of 1830, and asked to resign. Cumberland's graduates in 1829 were A. Delany, J. McCutcheon, F. E. Calhoon, J. A. Copp, and W. McBride. Only McCutcheon was a Kentuckian.[45]

Thomas Posey Street enrolled in Cumberland in 1829. This of itself is hardly remarkable. However, Street's letter home, published as "Cumberland College in 1829," provides one of the rare glimpses into student life at Cumberland College. Of one thing he was particularly proud, "It may give you some gratification to learn that I have quit chewing tobacco."[46]

At the same meeting that offered employment to the miserable Guerin, Franceway Cossitt was reengaged as President of Cumberland College. However, his salary was dropped by a considerable percentage to $833 per year. On the other hand, Daniel L. Morrison, assistant teacher, assumed the duties of Corresponding Secretary and Clerk of the Faculty and received a salary increase

---

[44]**Ibid.**

[45]Minutes of the Board of Trustees of Cumberland College, May 30, December 29, 1829, as recorded in Richard Beard's "Brief Historical Sketch of Cumberland College," 138-39, 171-72.

[46]Thomas P. Street, "Cumberland College in 1829," **Register of the Kentucky Historical Society**, 66 (October 1968), 392.

from $550 per year to $600.[47]

On January 27, 1830, David Lowry was employed as professor of moral philosophy. His salary was not assigned at this meeting but referred to the General Assembly. Franceway and Lucinda Cossitt's second daughter, Mary Ellen Cossitt, was born on August 1, 1830.[48]

Realizing the depth of the financial well Cumberland College was descending, the synod petitioned the Kentucky Legislature on October 24, 1828, asking them to pass into law authority for the collection of the pledges made in support of the college. Apparently, no such act was forthcoming. Financially exhausted, the trustees decided at their meeting of December 29, 1829, that the old pledges from the citizens of the Princeton area had to be collected. Toward this end,

> *Resolved*, That Will Lander be, and he is hereby, appointed a commissioner to collect the subscriptions to the Cumberland College, within Caldwell and adjacent counties; that the said commissioner be, and he is hereby, authorized to close the same by note, or notes with a credit of six or twelve months, and upon the failure or refusal of the subscribers to adjust their subscriptions within a reasonable time, according to the terms of the subscription, that then, and in that event, the said commissioner be required to collect the same by due course of law.[49]

However, according to Beard, "there is no account in the record of any assistance from the old subscriptions."[50]

As the financial situation of the college further deteriorated, continued efforts were made to collect fifty cents from every member

---

[47]Beard, "Brief Historical Sketch of Cumberland College," 139-40.

[48]**Ibid.**, 140.

[49]Minutes of Cumberland Synod of the Cumberland Presbyterian Church, October 24, 1828; Minutes of the Board of Trustees of Cumberland College, December 29, 1829, as recorded in Richard Beard's "Brief Historical Sketch of Cumberland College," 138-39.

[50]Beard, "Brief Historical Sketch of Cumberland College," 139.

of the denomination for its support. This effort began as dictated by Cumberland Synod on October 24, 1828, and was continued under the General Assembly of the Cumberland Presbyterian Church. A large number of ministers were each assigned a district in which to collect and all ministers were instructed to participate in the effort. However, very little money was ever actually gathered in this manner.[51]

After the formation of a General Assembly for the Cumberland Presbyterian Denomination in 1829, most matters dealing with Cumberland College fell under the jurisdiction of the Committee on Education. It was to this committee that the faculty presented their annual report and that memorials concerning the college were presented. As originally constituted, the Committee on Education consisted of Robert Donnell, David Foster, Alexander Chapman, James G. Guthrie, Samuel Harris, and R. E. C. Dougherty.[52]

Perhaps nervous over the tenuous financial situation of the college, the General Assembly at its first meeting instructed the trustees to "secure to themselves and their successors in office a legal title to the tract of land purchased for the benefit of said College." Also at this first General Assembly meeting, on May 23, 1829, Franceway Ranna Cossitt was appointed Stated Clerk of the General Assembly of the Cumberland Presbyterian Church. Cossitt was instructed by the assembly to "travel three or four months in the State of New York and elsewhere for the purpose of soliciting books and funds for the benefit of Cumberland College."[53]

It was at this time and in the interest of fund raising that Cossitt published **A Brief View of Cumberland College, Founded by the Synod of the Cumberland Presbyterian Church, near**

---

[51]Minutes of Cumberland Synod of the Cumberland Presbyterian Church, October 24, 1828; Minutes of the General Assembly of the Cumberland Presbyterian Church, May 20, 1829; May 19, 1830.

[52]Minutes of the General Assembly of the Cumberland Presbyterian Church, May 20-22, 1829.

[53]Minutes of the General Assembly of the Cumberland Presbyterian Church, May 23, 25, 1829.

Princeton, Kentucky. Although attributed to a committee of Cumberland Synod, Franceway Cossitt is generally acknowledged to have been the primary writer of this document; it is signed by him for the committee. **A Brief View of Cumberland College** was intended to promote the institution both in and out of the traditional area of the Cumberland Presbyterian Church.[54]

A Brief View of Cumberland College stressed those elements which Cossitt believed were most beneficial. Chief among these was Cumberland's position as a manual labor college with a farm attached to provided a constant source of student employment and to promote "corporal strength and mental energy." The schools devotion to the elimination of luxury, such as the often vilified feather beds, in order to develop "a strong constitution" was also stressed. Parents were urged to send no more money than actually necessary for expenses in order to teach the "judicious use of money."[55]

So, the system in use at Cumberland College was advertised to promote health of body, produce energy of mind, guard the morals and habits, provide for a season of adversity, reduce the expenses of an education, improve agriculture, and to give permanency to republican institutions. Cossitt said of his students "a considerable number are the sons of the most wealthy citizens; others the children of poor parents. But no one feels his *superiority;* no one his *inferiority*."[56]

Perhaps the most curious paragraph from **A Brief View of Cumberland College** is that which deals with the school's finances. "...with not more than eighty students, the College realized, from the last year's operation [1827], a clear profit, after defraying all the expenses of the establishment, which fully proves the practicability of the plan." Although the college farm's production apparently had been good during 1827, the claim that income had defrayed "all the expenses of the establishment" was either a gross misunderstanding

---

[54]Cossitt, **A Brief View of Cumberland College**, i.

[55]Ibid., 3.

[56]Ibid., 8-12.

of the actual situation a calculated deception. In the appendix of the same volume, Cossitt claims a debt of $5,000 for the college. Perhaps Franceway Cossitt's deep emotional involvement with Cumberland College clouded his judgement or, perhaps, it can be discounted as pure propaganda, but the fact remains that Cumberland College was never financially successful. By 1830, the General Assembly of the Cumberland Presbyterian Church was ready to reconsider the practicality of Cossitt's original plan.[57]

The degree to which Cossitt's involvement in Cumberland College stretched is clearly reflected in a letter written to his brother Ambrose Cossitt on November 22, 1828.

> This college owes its existence to me—this is acknowledged by all. I proposed the plan and the Synod adopted it. I have had a great share in its location, organization and progress. I look upon it with the eye of a parent, and as its President, my interests are identified with it.

Franceway stated, "my College which is the apple of eye to me (and such as it is) my reputation" and that he could probably remain president of the college "as long as I choose." He continued that it would have been unlikely that he could have risen to a similar *lucrative* position had he remained in his native New Hampshire.[58]

Between the first and second meetings of the General Assembly, Cossitt with David Lowry began publication of **The Religious and Literary Intelligencer**. By May of 1830, he was ready to turn this project over to someone else and readily agreed when the General Assembly suggested that it might entirely go into the hands of David Lowry. The assembly intended that Cossitt devote all of his time to the college. Cossitt agreed to write an article

---

[57]**Ibid.**, 4, 14; Minutes of the General Assembly of the Cumberland Presbyterian Church, May 20, 1830.

[58]Franceway Ranna Cossitt to Ambrose Cossitt, November 22, 1828.

explaining the change of editors.[59]

One result of the 1830 General Assembly's reconsideration of Cumberland College was the decision, made on Friday, May 21, 1830, that it was not practical to proceed with plans to establish a theological department attached to the college. On Monday, May 24, the decision was made to raise the tuition and board at Cumberland to $80 per academic year, to employ a separate manager for the boarding operation, and to employ a person as a farm hand to work with the students. The assembly also instructed that any trustee or employee that disagreed with these improvements was to be dismissed. This measure apparently prompted the immediate resignation of trustee John H. Phelps who was replaced by John Barnett.[60]

In 1830, the Committee on Education, now consisting of Finis Ewing, Robert Donnell, James Smith, James H. Walker, William S. Watterson, Benjamin Dechard, and Daniel L. Morrison, reported their findings,

> The Committee on Education have taken the subject into consideration and beg leave to report:
> That they have visited the several departments of Cumberland College and found them in the following condition:—The Faculty appear to have been diligent in attending to the instruction of the students: but it found that their labors have been much increased by the want of regular collegiate classes: it is, therefore, proposed that a regular classification of the students be made, that a preparatory school be established, and that this be done under the immediate direction of the Trustees. It is also recommended that the Trustees employ no professor or Tutor without the consent and approbation of the Faculty.
> In the refectory ample provision has been made for the diet of the students. They would recommend in this department a closer

---

[59]Minutes of the General Assembly of the Cumberland Presbyterian Church, May 20, 1830; Beard, "Brief Historical Sketch of Cumberland College," 142.

[60]Minutes of the General Assembly of the Cumberland Presbyterian Church, May 21, 24, 1830; Beard, "Brief Historical Sketch of Cumberland College," 142.

attention to economy, and suggest the suitableness of a cooking stove in preparing the various articles of food and, also that a greater quantity of milk be provided for the use of the students.

On the farm they have found the fences in good repair and the crops promising for the season.

They would recommend that a larger quantity of small grain be raised and that the superintendent be directed to turn his attention more to the cultivation of clover and the preparation of grass lots. The committee are gratified to report that the students profess to be well satisfied. Every room has been visited by them, and they have found the students from the different states in which they have resided, in the enjoyment of excellent health, and satisfied with the board and pleased with the labor. They have heard no complaints from the students, though they were requested to make known any grievance that might exist, and, amongst more than one hundred and twenty students, but one case of bodily indisposition was found and that was slight.

These circumstances together abundantly prove the utility of the plan of embracing mutual labor, in the open air, with those studies which require confinement. The institution has been extensively useful in disseminating useful knowledge: but from the low price of board which has heretofore been required, a large debt has been contracted. From the proposed plan, however, of increasing the price to a fair equivalent, they are of the opinion that the College will be fully adequate to its own support: and they recommend that the energies of all your preachers be employed in bringing forward efficient cooperation from the people, to extinguish that debt which has already been contracted.

All of which is respectfully submitted.

Robert Donnell, Chairman[61]

From this report it can be seen that overall the committee was pleased with the operation of the college. In fact, the only exceptions seem to have fallen into the area of fiscal management. As this report stated, it was hoped that raising tuition and board from $60 to $80 per year would enable Cumberland College to operate profitably. This, however, proved not to be the case. Still, if student satisfaction was

---

[61]Minutes of the General Assembly of the Cumberland Presbyterian Church, May 24, 1830.

any measure, then the college was at least in part successful.[62]

Early in 1830, the publication of the Cumberland Presbyterian denomination's first periodical, **Religious and Literary Intelligencer**, began in Princeton, Kentucky. Loosely connected with Cumberland College and edited by Franceway Cossitt for the first few months of its existence, this publication saw editorial control transferred to David Lowry. Later it became the **Revivalist** and, later still, the **Cumberland Presbyterian**.[63]

Perhaps our best picture of Cumberland College as it was in the early 1830s comes from Richard Beard's *Brief Historical Sketch of Cumberland College, at Princeton*, published in the **Theological Medium, A Cumberland Presbyterian Quarterly** in the April, 1876, issue. Beard, a freshman in 1830, remembers this period fondly. When he arrived on campus, Cossitt, Morrison, and Guerin, were the teachers. Morrison, however, left at the end of the year. F. C. Usher and "a young Mr. Dodds" were preparatory teachers. John McGrew managed the dormitories and Rainer Mercer managed the farm. There were about 125 students at the time.

> The college seemed a good deal like a bee-hive. Each teacher was ringing the bell every hour for his class; and every two hours the horn was blowing for the laboring divisions. All seemed to be interest and animation. It must be confessed, however, that a portion of the animation, and a portion by no means inconsiderable, as time showed, was expended in mischief: but still there was life. In addition to all, the faculty, dressed in their long black gowns, presented rather an imposing appearance to a frontier circuit-rider and common school teacher. The black gowns, however, it is believed, did not outlive that collegiate year.[64]

The graduating class of 1830 consisted of Cornelius G. McPherson and James P. Barnett. Of course, at that time it was necessary to replace Daniel L. Morrison, the assistant teacher. The

---

[62]Beard, "Brief Historical Sketch of Cumberland College," 142.

[63]Ibid., 177-78.

[64]Ibid., 141-42.

Board of Trustees addressed the issue on October 29, 1830, appointing Thomas C. Anderson as a tutor for one year. As compensation Anderson was to be paid $500. This engagement is also significant in that he was also expected to act as librarian. At the end of his appointment, Anderson's contract was renewed for a second year.[65]

Several items of interest took place at the meeting of the Board of Trustees of Cumberland College on April 2, 1831. John W. Ogden turned over $700 collected by him in the name of the college. Unfortunately this is the only record of a significant contribution raised by any of the missionaries. Desperate to do something about the school's financial situation before the meeting of the General Assembly in May, a proposal was entertained to mortgage some of Cumberland's property in order to raise $3,000. A proposition was made by Hiram McDaniel, John Barnett, and Franceway Cossitt that they would each donate $100 toward the institution's debts if 47 others could be convinced to do the same. Apparently, nothing came of either proposal.[66]

On May 18, 1831, the General Assembly of the Cumberland Presbyterian Church demanded that the Trustees of Cumberland College make "a report of the true state of the College" including all of their financial records. By this time Franceway R. Cossitt was putting pressure on the assembly for payment of funds due him for his services at the college. To settle this the assembly ordered that David Lowry pay Cossitt out of the profits of the **Religious and Literary Intelligencer**. Despite the financial situation, the assembly recommended that the trustees employ "a proper professor or professors in the departments of science." Two trustees, Elijah Shepherdson and Colonel John M. Burke, were appointed to the board and two others, John H. Racherby and Robert A. Patterson, had

---

[65]Minutes of the Board of Trustees of Cumberland College, October 29, 1830, as reported in Richard Beard's "Brief Historical Sketch of Cumberland College," 142-43.

[66]Minutes of the Board of Trustees of Cumberland College, April 2, 1831, as reported in Richard Beard's "Brief Historical Sketch of Cumberland College," 143.

previous board appointments confirmed.[67]

The assembly was nearing desperation over Cumberland's finances. A Committee of Arrangements for Cumberland College was appointed on May 22, 1831. This committee consisted of William Harris, Robert Donnell, Franceway Cossitt, Reuben Burrow, James McReynolds, John Vining, and William S. Watterson. These men were to deal with the issues surrounding the college's debt and recommend action to the assembly.[68]

The best solution that seemed to present itself was that of two ministers, John Barnett and Aaron Shelby. It stated,

> On condition that the members of the Assembly will give their notes to the amount of two thousand four hundred dollars, payable one-half next May, and the other half in May 1833, the said Barnett and Shelby will assume the payment of all the debts of the college of whatever kind or character existing at this date. Provided furthermore:
>
> 1. That the net profits of the printing office belong to the said Barnett and Shelby, for the term of four years from this date, together with the profits of the past year.
>
> 2. That after the current expenses of Cumberland College are paid, the net profits arising from tuition, as they may be ascertained, belong to said Barnett and Shelby, for the four years next ensuing.
>
> 3. That all monies now on hands, not otherwise appropriated, either in the treasury or the hands of individuals, together with all subscriptions, bonds, deeds (except the College deed), notes, accounts, etc., be given to said Barnett and Shelby.
>
> 4. That the two brick-kilns belonging to Cumberland College, be given to said Barnett and Shelby.
>
> 5. That all monies now, or hereafter collected by Rev. John W. Ogden, not otherwise now appropriated, belong to said Barnett and Shelby, and that some one missionary be employed to make

---

[67]Minutes of the General Assembly of the Cumberland Presbyterian Church, May 18, 21-22, 1831.

[68]Minutes of the General Assembly of the Cumberland Presbyterian Church, May 22, 1831.

collections for four years.[69]

Barnett and Shelby were required to accept the following conditions,

> 1. That the General Assembly under this contract, have the paramount control of Cumberland College as heretofore.
> 2. That the Trustees have power to appoint officers and make contracts for the regulation of the literary, farming and boarding departments as heretofore and to transact all other business, for which they are empowered in the charter, not interfering with this contract.[70]

This contract was accepted precipitating the resignation of John Barnett as a trustee of Cumberland College. David M. McGoodwin was immediately appointed to fill the vacant position. Perhaps still nervous about their position, the General Assembly ordered Hiram McDaniel and Richard Beard to investigate the financial status of the **Religious and Literary Intelligencer**. Nothing connected with Cumberland College could be presumed to be debt free.[71]

The concept behind this plan was that the management of Cumberland College had been somehow faulty and that under the direction of men more experienced in business the financial situation could be reversed. For their part, Barnett and Shelby thought that they risked little because the General Assembly had agreed to collect promises of financial support from among its ministers. Franceway Cossitt and Samuel D. Hawk were placed in charge of collecting these pledges. As usual, very little money was ever actually

---

[69]Minutes of the General Assembly of the Cumberland Presbyterian Church, May 23, 1831; Beard, "Brief Historical Sketch of Cumberland College," 144-45.

[70]Minutes of the General Assembly of the Cumberland Presbyterian Church, May 23, 1831; Beard, "Brief Historical Sketch of Cumberland College," 145.

[71]Minutes of the General Assembly of the Cumberland Presbyterian Church, May 23, 1831; Beard, "Franceway Ranna Cossitt," 159-161.

collected.[72]

Thomas C. Anderson and Franceway Cossitt were the only instructors employed to the end of the 1831-1832 academic year. It can be supposed that they were ample to the task. Enrollment had dropped since tuition and board were raised to $80 per year. Four students graduated in 1831, Thomas B. Reynolds, R. S. Dulin, R. B. Castleman, and Amos Andrews.[73]

After the first quarter of 1832, the Trustees of Cumberland College were again ready to expand the faculty as they had been requested by the General Assembly at its last meeting. At the meeting of the trustees on April 30, 1832, Livingston Lindsey was appointed professor of mathematics and natural philosophy. His appointment was for one year and carried a stipend of $550. Lindsey received most of his education at the University of Virginia. He remained on the faculty of Cumberland College until 1838.[74]

The graduates of 1832 included C. W. Ridgeley, W. G. Estill, William Barnett, and Richard Beard. Barnett studied medicine and returned to the area of Princeton to practice. Thomas C. Anderson severed his connection with Cumberland at the end of the 1832 school year. He was rewarded for his service with the honorary degree of Bachelor of Arts. On the day after commencement, Richard Beard was appointed professor of languages to replace Anderson. His stipend was $500 per year.[75]

The meeting of General Assembly in 1832, saw James B. Porter, Hugh Kirkpatrick, James S. Guthrie, Albert G. Gibson, John Morgan, Franceway R. Cossitt, John L. Dillard, Thomas B. Wilson, John Bell, and William Moore appointed to the Committee on

---

[72]Minutes of the General Assembly of the Cumberland Presbyterian Church, May 23, 1831; Beard, "Brief Historical Sketch of Cumberland College," 145.

[73]Beard, "Brief Historical Sketch of Cumberland College," 145.

[74]Minutes of the Board of Trustees of Cumberland College, April 30, 1832, as reported in Richard Beard's "Brief Historical Sketch of Cumberland College," 146-47.

[75]Beard, "Brief Historical Sketch of Cumberland College," 146.

Education. Mr. Welde, a representative of a group of supporters of manual labor institutions from the state of New York addressed the assembly on Friday, May 18, and was widely approved. Franceway Cossitt was instructed to aid him in gathering information about Cumberland College. Further, the period of Christmas vacation was adjusted to last from mid-December through the month of January.[76]

The 1832 assembly addressed the need for frugality at the college, instructing the trustees to arrange for lectures at least once a month on the subject of *economy*. This move was precipitated by complaints of extravagance made by the parents of students. In the opinion of the assembly, "this seems to be the principal objection on the public mind against the institution."[77] At their meeting of June 25, 1832, the Board of Trustees passed the following resolution intended to promote a dress code, of sorts, for Cumberland College.

> Whereas, The General Assembly of the Cumberland Presbyterian Church, held in May last, in Nashville, adopted a resolution recommending to the trustees of Cumberland College, to pass some ordinance, more effectively to preserve economy among the students, whilst members of said institution; therefore on motion of J. H. Rackerby,
>
> *Resolved*, That in future the students and faculty of said college be, and are hereby advised to wear as their weekly apparel during winter, good strong woolen jeans, or cassinette; and for summer, flax linen, or hemp linen, or some article of domestic manufacture, so as to secure the object contemplated by the General Assembly; also that each student be requested to furnish himself with a large and strong linen apron, which may be used when at work, so as to preserve his other clothes.[78]

----

[76]Minutes of the General Assembly of the Cumberland Presbyterian Church, May 16, 18-19, 1832.

[77]Minutes of the General Assembly of the Cumberland Presbyterian Church, May 18, 22, 1832.

[78]Minutes of the Board of Trustees of Cumberland College, June 25, 1832, as reported in Richard Beard's "Brief Historical Sketch of Cumberland College," 147.

Cumberland's financial situation was not ignored by the 1832 assembly. Franceway Cossitt was instructed to write a circular letter detailing the financial situation and other problems of the college. This letter was intended to spur presbyterial involvement in recruiting students and soliciting donations for the college. Also, patronage for the **Religious and Literary Intelligencer** was to be stressed. David Lowry was appointed to have the letter published and distributed.[79]

Several adjustments to the agreement with Barnett and Shelby were made. In exchange for an extension on their lease on the rest of the college property to seven years from October 15, 1831, Barnett and Shelby were asked to give up their claim to the printing press and the profits from it. They were also promised that if the profits of the college and the indemnity given by the trustees failed to meet the institutions debts, then a portion of the college property could be liquidated to defray the balance of debt. Capital expenditures for "permanent and useful buildings" were to be permitted and compensated by further extensions to the lease. By 1833, the lease had been extended to twelve years with the provision that it could be bought out at a rate of $300 per year. The General Assembly stressed that they expected to receive Cumberland College debt free at the end of Barnett and Shelby's lease. In order to eliminate the institution's debts, Barnett and Shelby secured a loan from the Bank of the United States.[80]

On April 19, 1833, the trustees entered into an agreement with Barnett and Shelby for the construction of a new main building for the college. When finished, according to Richard Beard, the building had "the appearance of a Pennsylvania barn." It was a two-story brick construction 65 feet long by 39 feet wide providing eight blocks of rooms. On the second floor, lighted by dormer windows, were two library rooms and the college chapel. According to witnesses, the rooms were comfortable but, "the roof, lower floors, gable ends, fireplaces, hearths, and probably some other parts, are not done in a

---

[79]Minutes of the General Assembly of the Cumberland Presbyterian Church, May 19, 1832.

[80]Minutes of the General Assembly of the Cumberland Presbyterian Church, May 19, 1832, May 22, 1833.

sufficient workmanship-like manner." According to Beard, "the great object was to provide comfortable lodgings for the students as well as rooms to study." Some of the rooms were used for lectures on occasion. The chapel was used for classes as well as services.[81]

In 1833 and 1834, the agreement made with Barnett and Shelby seemed to be operating smoothly. The General Assembly of 1833, has little to say of Cumberland College except to voice their satisfaction with the arrangement and to appoint missionaries to collect funds as they were obligated by the lease. In the fall of 1833, Shelby sold his interest in Cumberland College to Harvey Young. Young and his family moved to the campus to manage the farm and boarding establishment. This transfer was recognized by default by the assembly in 1834.[82]

In 1833, the graduating class consisted of Cyrus Haynes, William A. Scott, Richard Henry Ball, Lawrence N. Waddill, G. W. Smith, A. S. Mitchell, and Jesse Franklin Ford. Only William Scott entered the Cumberland Presbyterian ministry. The class of 1834, had two members, Pleasant M. Griffin and John A. Hanson. Griffin was sponsored in his ministerial education by the Cumberland Presbyterian congregation of Winchester, Tennessee, but he died within a year of entering the ministry.[83]

In 1833, Andrew Jackson, Jr., adopted son of then United States President Andrew Jackson, appeared on the roll of Cumberland College. Andrew Jackson, Jr., was one of the twin sons of Rachel Jackson's brother, Severn Donelson, and was adopted by the president the day he was born. "Since both of his parents were alive at the time of his adoption, the reason he was given to them is not clear." The president's son had a reputation for fast living and unpaid debts. He appeared on the roll of Cumberland College for only one

---

[81] Beard, "Brief Historical Sketch of Cumberland College," 148; Minutes of the General Assembly of the Cumberland Presbyterian Church, May 25, 1835.

[82] Minutes of the General Assembly of the Cumberland Presbyterian Church, May 22, 25, 1833, May 23, 1834; Beard, "Brief Historical Sketch of Cumberland College," 148.

[83] Beard, "Brief Historical Sketch of Cumberland College," 147-50.

37

year and it is unclear if he ever actually set foot on the campus. Surely the presence of such a celebrity would have elicited comments in the church press. It also seems likely that Jackson's fellow students would have made comments and that at least some of them would have survived. Finally, the brief existence of another Cumberland College in Nashville potentially adds to the confusion.[84]

---

[84]"Treasurer's Book of Cumberland College;" "First Lady Biography: Rachel Jackson," National First Ladies Library, retrieved February 17, 2007, from http://www.firstladies.org/.

CHOLERA

Early in November, 1832, cholera first appeared in the area of Princeton. Cossitt wrote, "The Cholera has been in town. There have been two deaths." The area would not be completely free of the disease or the afflictions associated with it until about 1835. Fear swept the campus of Cumberland College in 1832, but no outbreak of the disease occurred there immediately and the college continued operation without disruption of the daily routine. Death, however, seemed to settle on the campus. The first death recorded was that of Lucinda Cossitt. In surviving records, no cause of death was ever attributed and her husband insisted that his school remained free of the disease, however, Lucinda would probably have been in her early-thirties at the time of her death. While the exact date of her death is not recorded, Richard Beard preached her funeral sermon on Sunday, March 17, 1833.[85]

Cossitt found himself without a spouse raising four children, one son (Asbury Haspending) and three daughters (Anne Catherine, Mary Ellen, and Lucinda Louise born in about 1832), all less than ten years old. On January 19, 1834, Franceway Cossitt remarried. His new wife, Elkton's Matilda Edwards, was an acquaintance from the brief period of his residence there. Cossitt had been a widower for less than a year. While in Princeton one of Cossitt's daughters, Susan, also died. As to the exact date of both her birth and death the record is silent. However, it is likely that Susan Cossitt was born about 1831 and it is possible that her death was associated with the cholera in about 1833. It is also possible that Susan died in infancy before the

---

[85]Beard, "Brief Historical Sketch of Cumberland College," 148-49; Nancy D. Baird, "Asiatic Cholera's First Visit to Kentucky: A Study in Panic and Fear," **Filson Club History Quarterly**, 48 (1974), 228; Franceway Ranna Cossitt to Rodrick Horton, November 26, 1832; Richard Beard, "Funeral Sermon, Occasioned by the Death of Mrs. Lucinda Cossitt, Consort of the Rev. F. R. Cossitt, President of Cumberland College, and Delivered at the Request of the Deceased. Princeton, Ky, Sabbath, March 17, 1833," **Cumberland Presbyterian Pulpit**, I (May, 1833), 63; Beard, "Franceway Ranna Cossitt," 178.

cholera hit Princeton.[86]

Summer 1834, saw the return of cholera. Richard Beard remembered that the disease broke out in Princeton about July 1. Again, at first, the disease did not reach the college, isolated as it was, about a mile from the town. Soon, however, the disease did develop at Cumberland. Many of the students and faculty were stricken. James P. Barnett, John Barnett's eldest son, and Harvey Young died. The disease lingered for weeks. Those of the 88 enrolled students who were close enough to home or who had friends in the area fled. At least one unnamed student who remained died. The college lost entire semester and, most importantly, the income from the semester. Unfortunately, after the danger was past many of the students that fled the disease did not return. Enrollment for the semester after the cholera was 65 students.[87]

One of the issues addressed by the meeting of the General Assembly in 1835, was the rumor spreading through the church that Cumberland College was not a healthy place. Such a story could have proven to be disastrous to the institution. The Committee on Education consisting of Jacob Lindly, Robert Donnell, J. C. Mitchell, R. L. Caruthers, and D. L. Morrison, stated,

> there is no cause perceivable by them to induce the belief that the College will in the future be more liable to the visitation of disease than the most salubrious situation in the Western country. . . no institution in the West has better prospects of health.

The committee went on to claim that cholera had never actually visited Cumberland College and that, rather, the deaths there could be contributed to a "congestive fever." This deception was, no doubt, a further attempt to restore public faith in the college. As another attempt to remove the fear of disease, it was recommended to change the time of the college's major vacation from Christmas, during

---

[86]Beard, "Franceway Ranna Cossitt," 178; "Cossitt Family Information."

[87]Beard, "Brief Historical Sketch of Cumberland College," 149; Beard, "Franceway Ranna Cossitt," 161; Minutes of the General Assembly of the Cumberland Presbyterian Church, May 25, 1835.

December and January, to summer, when the danger of disease was greatest.[88]

After Young's death, the Board of Trustees entered into an agreement with John Barnett to replace him in the fiscal management of the college. The Committee on Education noted this change in 1835. The necessity for this action was stated to be that "there is yet a considerable debt against the institution." This acknowledgment ended any impression that Cumberland College's financial problems were over. The General Assembly urged each presbytery to endow one or more scholarships.[89]

Robert Taylor, John Polk, Joseph Kirkpatrick, Cyrus Harnes, and Robert L. Caruthers were appointed by the 1835 assembly to "review and examine the college edifice, and report the workmanship and quality of the materials." This committee made the first extensive report on the college since the beginning of the lease arrangement.

> Your committee cannot refrain from expressing their approbation of the evidence which the Trustees bear in their report, to the high qualifications of the President and Professors of the College, and the faithful manner in which they have performed their duties. They feel entirely free to recommend them in the highest terms to this Assembly and the public, as well qualified to perform the duties required of them.

The committee also found the farm to be in acceptable condition. However, they must have believed that a greater degree of accountability was necessary. The committee instructed the president and professors to report the origin and progress of the college including future prospects. The Board of Trustees was also instructed to make an annual report to the General Assembly including the

---

[88]Minutes of the General Assembly of the Cumberland Presbyterian Church, May 20, 25, 1835; Minutes of the Commission to Relocate Cumberland College, March 1, 1843, as recorded in **Banner of Peace and Cumberland Presbyterian Advocate** 2 (March 10, 1843), 2-3.

[89]Beard, "Brief Historical Sketch of Cumberland College," 150; Minutes of the General Assembly of the Cumberland Presbyterian Church, May 25, 1835.

status of the institution's debts.[90]

The authority of the Board of Trustees was further curbed by the passing of a resolution which stated, "that the Board of Trustees of Cumberland College, can only be appointed by the General Assembly of the Cumberland Presbyterian Church." Elijah Shepherdson and William Mercer were appointed to fill vacancies on the board. However, they had already begun serving in that capacity at the board's request.[91]

Increasing displeasure and doubt about Rev. John Barnett's ability as a manager began to make themselves felt at about this same time. According to Beard, "some thought he managed badly; others thought he managed wholly with a view to his own selfish ends; others went so far as to impeach his integrity as a man of business and a Christian."[92]

Three men, J. H. Whetstone, T. J. Houghton, and W. J. Houghton, graduated in December of 1835. In 1836, with graduation moved to July, J. R. Denton, J. S. Roane, John C. Kirkpatrick, G. W. Usher, W. E. Barnett, J. W. Taylor, and J. M. Taylor received their degrees. An honorary degree was also presented to D. R. Harris in 1836.[93]

By 1836, the ire of the assembly fell squarely on the Board of Trustees of Cumberland College for assuming Harvey Young's portion of the lease agreement. This action, the Committee on the Subject of Cumberland College pointed out, had been taken without the consent of the assembly and was ill advised. They continued, "the whole concern appears to be exceedingly embarrassed, and the Faculty and managers are in an unpleasant situation." By this time the

---

[90]Minutes of the General Assembly of the Cumberland Presbyterian Church, May 22, 25, 1835.

[91]Minutes of the General Assembly of the Cumberland Presbyterian Church, May 25, 1835.

[92]Beard, "Franceway Ranna Cossitt," 161.

[93]Beard, "Brief Historical Sketch of Cumberland College," 150.

approximate debt of Cumberland was $9,000.[94]

This was the first year that the Committee on the Subject of Cumberland College or, as it was more often referenced, the Committee on the College existed. It is quite likely that the Committee on Education became the Committee on the College when that institution was to be discussed. Members were Jacob Lindley, Robert Donnell, J. C. Mitchell, R. L. Caruthers, D. L. Morrison, H. H. Hill and [Reuben?] Burrow.[95]

As a solution, this committee suggested that a voluntary association be formed to assume all responsibility for Cumberland College from John Barnett. The association would pay the first $7,000 of Cumberland's debt and Barnett, the rest. In return ownership of Cumberland College and all property attached to it would be transferred to the Cumberland College Association. This proposal was signed by Robert Donnell for the committee and accepted by John Barnett. On Monday morning, May 23, 1836, the recommended association was reported having been formed.[96]

However, the Cumberland College Association was not able to take control of the college in 1836. Rather, the combined administration of Barnett and the Board of Trustees continued into 1837. In 1837, at the meeting of General Assembly, William Harris, J. L. Smith, William R. Martin, Joel Lambert, Jacob Fisher, H. A. Hunter, and J. D. Porter were appointed to be the Committee on the College. They reported that the Cumberland College Association had not been able to take possession of the college property due to

---

[94]Minutes of the General Assembly of the Cumberland Presbyterian Church, May 21, 1836.

[95]Minutes of the General Assembly of the Cumberland Presbyterian Church, May 20, 1835, May 20, 1836.

[96]Minutes of the General Assembly of the Cumberland Presbyterian Church, May 21, 1836; Minutes of the Commission to Relocate Cumberland College, March 1, 1843, as recorded in **Banner of Peace and Cumberland Presbyterian Advocate** 2 (March 10, 1843), 2-3.

complications in the legal status of the institution.[97]

In the year between meetings, the debt of Cumberland College had risen to $12,000. The committee pointed out,

> the only way in which Barnett is liable for his portion of them [the college's debts], is upon his contract with the Trustees. Thus it will be seen that the Trustees may be sued upon the notes given by them for debts contracted by the firm; judgements recovered, and executions leveled, and the property sold; and the whole debt made out of them, when according to their contract, they ought not to pay but half, and their only recourse on Barnett will be to sue him upon his contract; and before this can be done the College property may be sacrificed.

Matters were further complicated. A few days before entering into contract with the trustees, Barnett had mortgaged his interest in the college property to Henry Machew and "others" along with "his land upon which he lives, his household and kitchen furniture, his horses, cattle and hogs." Clearly, Barnett's financial situation appeared as dire as the college's. While faulting the trustees for getting themselves into this situation, the committee exonerated them. The trustees had, the committee determined, "acted solely with a view to the interest of the institution."[98]

The physical examination of Cumberland College in 1837, found the farm in excellent condition. The refectory, under the management of Mr. Kendrick, was reported to be "well conducted." The college buildings, however, were not greeted with enthusiasm.

> The large edifice erected under the contract with Barnett and Shelby, has not been finished according to contract. With the exception of the foundation, the building is of indifferent materials. On the outside, the holes left to make scaffolding, have not been filled, nor the house penciled. The pavements in the passages have

---

[97]Beard, "Brief Historical Sketch of Cumberland College," 151; Beard, "Franceway Ranna Cossitt," 161; Minutes of the General Assembly of the Cumberland Presbyterian Church, May 17, 23, 1837.

[98]Minutes of the General Assembly of the Cumberland Presbyterian Church, May 23, 1837.

not been laid; the roof is very indifferent, and in short, there is no part of it finished according to contract, with the exception of the above mentioned.

Still, the committee placed no blame on the faculty, only on John Barnett.[99]

As in 1836, the Committee on the College in 1837, pointed to the formation of an association as a solution to Cumberland College's financial problems. Another committee, made up of John W. Ogden, John Morgan, and A. McDowell, was instructed to confer with John Barnett to see if he was willing to give up his interest in the college. Still another committee, members unnamed, was instructed to determine if the formation of an "Association of individuals" to relieve the school was possible. They quickly reported that it was. A joint stock company, Cumberland College Association was formed on May 25, 1837, and held its first meeting on May 26.[100]

---

[99]Minutes of the General Assembly of the Cumberland Presbyterian Church, May 23, 1837.

[100]Minutes of the General Assembly of the Cumberland Presbyterian Church, May 23, 1837; Beard, "Franceway Ranna Cossitt," 161; Beard, "Brief Historical Sketch of Cumberland College," 151-52.

CUMBERLAND COLLEGE ASSOCIATION

The General Assembly moved rapidly toward the establishment of the Cumberland College Association's control. The Board of Trustees of Cumberland College were instructed to transfer all title to the college property to the association. This action took place at the meeting of the Board of Trustees on May 29, 1837, and is reflected in the minutes;

> **Whereas**, The General Assembly of the Cumberland Presbyterian Church, at their late sessions in Princeton, in May, 1837, passed a resolution requiring the Board of Trustees of Cumberland College to transfer and convey all the college property, both real and personal, to an association of individuals thereafter to be formed, upon the condition that said association, when formed, shall assume and pay all debts and demands against said college not exceeding, however, the sum of twelve thousand dollars ($12,000); and, whereas, said association has since been formed, and have stipulated the fulfillment of their part of the engagement required by the said General Assembly; therefore, on motion of P. B. McGoodwin,
>
> *Resolved*, That the President of the Board, in his corporate capacity, be directed to execute and sign the necessary instrument or covenant by which all the property of said college, whether real or personal, which they hold as trustees, may be fully and effectually transferred and conveyed to the association aforesaid.[101]

The Association, for their part, agreed to take charge of all of the institution's debts, stating their belief that the college was, "of great public benefit, and of vital importance to the community, in which it is located, to the world, and to the Church." The assembly further instructed the trustees to petition the Kentucky legislature to alter the charter they had granted Cumberland College to reflect the

---

[101]Minutes of the General Assembly of the Cumberland Presbyterian Church, May 23, 1837; Minutes of the Board of Trustees of Cumberland College, May 29, 1837, as reported in Richard Beard's "Brief Historical Sketch of Cumberland College," 152.

new status.[102]

The General Assembly of the Commonwealth of Kentucky granted this petition on February 16, 1838. Recognizing debt as the reason for the change, the legislature ruled that the,

> association of individuals, under the name and style of "Cumberland College Association," is hereby invested with all the right, title and interest to the property, both real and personal, belonging to, or in anywise connected with, Cumberland College, which is now vested, by the charter of incorporation, in the "Trustees of the Cumberland College;" and that all assignments, transfers and conveyances of property, chooses in action, accounts, debts, claims, dues, and demands, which have hereto-fore, or may hereafter be made by the Trustees to the said association, shall be good and valid in law and equity.[103]

In order to protect the association and to prevent Cumberland College from accumulating debt indefinitely, the General Assembly of the Cumberland Presbyterian Church ruled that if, "after a fair trial, it [Cumberland College] shall prove to be a losing concern, then the Association shall be permitted to dispose of said establishment in any manner they may think proper." This statement provided the association with a means of escape; Cumberland College could be abandoned and the property sold, if it did not prove to be profitable.[104]

The seventeen articles of the Constitution of the Cumberland College Association provided for the issue of $40,000 in stock. Each

---

[102]Minutes of the General Assembly of the Cumberland Presbyterian Church, May 23, 1837; "Preamble to the Constitution of the Cumberland College Association," quoted in Richard Beard's "Brief Historical Sketch of Cumberland College," 153.

[103]"An Act to Amend the Charter of Cumberland College, and for other Purposes," Acts of the Legislature of the Commonwealth of Kentucky, relating to Incorporating Cumberland College of Princeton, Kentucky, February 16, 1838.

[104]Minutes of the General Assembly of the Cumberland Presbyterian Church, May 23, 1837.

share had a value of $200 which was to be paid by the owner into the association's treasury as the need arose. There was no limit set to the number of shares that could be purchased by any individual. One share, however, was all that was required to be a member of the association.[105]

Article fifteen of the constitution provided a clear statement of the association's objective, "the liquidation and settlement of the existing debts against the institution." After this goal was accomplished, funds could be used in any manner that a majority of the subscribers to the constitution saw fit.[106]

On formation the association's members were 34 representing 32 shares. Members included Joel Lambert, Thomas Lambert, C. P. Reed, James Smith, William L. Martin, T. C. Anderson, Thomas B. Wilson, J. C. Wear, John W. Ogden, F. C. Usher, Joseph Brown, and James Orr. Three other shares were held by unnamed Cumberland Presbyterians. Seventeen shares were held by interested non-Cumberland Presbyterians.[107]

As had been hoped so often in the past, the salvation of Cumberland College seemed at hand. In 1838, the General Assembly formed a new committee, Committee on Report of Cumberland Association, to deal with the college. Members included Robert Donnell, William Harris, W. S. Watterson, Jacob Fisher, H. B. Warren, Reuben Burrow, and James Wallace. After reviewing the report of the Cumberland College Association, the committee reported, "that the period has at last arrived we may consider her [Cumberland College] as established upon a solid basis." The assembly approved the appointment of James Smith, Thomas B. Wilson, Joel Lambert, Carson P. Reed, John W. Ogden, Joseph Brown, Franceway R. Cossitt, William McGowan, J. H. Rackerby, P. B. McGoodwin, W. P. Fowler. T. J. Flourney, and T. L. McNairy as

---

[105]Constitution of the Cumberland College Association, quoted in Richard Beard's "Brief Historical Sketch of Cumberland College," 153; Evans, "Cumberland Presbyterian Colleges," 84.

[106]Constitution of the Cumberland College Association, quoted in Richard Beard's "Brief Historical Sketch of Cumberland College," 153-54.

[107]Beard, "Brief Historical Sketch of Cumberland College," 154.

the new trustees of the college.[108]

This committee was the first to deal with the complaints of John Barnett over what he perceived to be his mistreatment at the hands of the General Assembly. It was Barnett's contention that his participation in the lease agreement had left him ruined financially. Further, he believed that either the association or the General Assembly owed him compensation. The assembly insisted that the matter be settled between Barnett and the college, "in accordance with the original engagement." On May 19, 1838, Barnett withdrew his complaint only to present it again to the 1840 assembly but with little more success. James Smith alone voted that Barnett might have grounds for a claim on the assembly. After being petitioned by Barnett again in 1841, the General Assembly ruled, "it is improper for this ecclesiastical body to adjudicate in the case."[109]

John Barnett, however, was not satisfied by this decision. He brought his position before the General Assembly again in 1842. On May 23, 1842, LeRoy Woods reported for the committee formed exclusively to deal with Barnett. The committee report consisted of the entire history of Barnett's complaint and reflected the assembly's growing exasperation with him and his financial problems and sustained the decisions of previous assemblies. It finally concluded,

> Your Committee would also sincerely hope and affectionately advise, that said Barnett, in view of his ordination vows, and under the influence of that heavenly and divine principle which beareth all things, will trouble the General Assembly no more upon that subject. And that reflections thrown from all parties may come to a perpetual end, and that the unfortunate difficulties connected therewith be buried in final oblivion.[110]

The graduates of 1837, included J. G. Biddle who was already

_____

[108]**Ibid.**, 154; Minutes of the General Assembly of the Cumberland Presbyterian Church, May 16-17, 1838.

[109]Minutes of the General Assembly of the Cumberland Presbyterian Church, May 17-19, 1838, May 25, 1840, May 25, 1841.

[110]Minutes of the General Assembly of the Cumberland Presbyterian Church, May 23, 1842.

a licentiate in the Cumberland Presbyterian Church, Stephen F. Hale, and Benjamin G. Dudley. In 1838, two men, Robert D. Ray and Thomas Johnson Phelps graduated from Cumberland College.[111]

During the summer break of 1838, Richard Beard was offered a position at Sharon College in Mississippi, which he accepted. He was replaced as professor of languages by F. C. Usher. Usher's connection to Cumberland College stretched back to before 1830. He had served as a prepatory teacher and was a member of the Cumberland College Association. After three years of study, Usher had graduated from Princeton Theological Seminary in New Jersey. At the same time, Livingston Lindsey ended his association with the college to become a lawyer in Princeton. Lindsey was eventually succeeded by Mr. Payne, a local Episcopal Minister, who remained with Cumberland for between twelve and eighteen months. After the 1840 meeting of the Cumberland Presbyterian General Assembly in May, Cornelius G. McPherson was appointed to teach "Mathematics and Natural Philosophy." McPherson, a member of the 1830 graduating class, stayed with Cumberland College in Princeton until 1842.[112]

[111]Beard, "Brief Historical Sketch of Cumberland College," 154-55.

[112]**Ibid.**, 155-57.

PRINCETON'S DECLINE

Despite the apparent improvement in Cumberland College's situation after the formation of the Cumberland College Association, the general impression of the Princeton population was that the Cumberland Presbyterian Church was distancing itself from the college. This belief prevented any extended financial participation by the population in the institution.[113]

Cumberland College Association's financial success did not last for very long. This attempt to save the college which, at first seemed so vital, quickly slowed. On January 3, 1839, a call was made on the stock of the association. Each share required a payment of $70. On April 4, 1839, the Association made a loan from the Bank of Hopkinsville for $1000 in order to pay the most immediate expenses of the college. By April 22, 1839, the association was, "under imperious necessity of raising $3047.50 to pay certain debts." Loans were secured but the interest demanded was as high as twenty percent.[114]

Because there was to be no meeting of the General Assembly in 1839, a convention of the church was called. This convention took place in Nashville from May 21 to 25, 1839. Franceway Cossitt attended as the representative of Cumberland College. On Wednesday morning, May 22, the convention stated that, "the condition of said institution [Cumberland College] appears to be better than at any former period." Cossitt managed to keep news of the still deteriorating financial situation at Cumberland College from

---

[113]Beard, "Franceway Ranna Cossitt," 162.

[114]Minutes of the Board of Directors of the Cumberland College Association, January 2, 1839, April 22, 1839, as recorded in Henry Bascom Evans, "History of the Organization and Administration of Cumberland Presbyterian Colleges" (Ph.D. dissertation, George Peabody College for Teachers, 1938), 84.

the delegates to the convention.[115]

Shortly after the convention adjourned, however, Franceway Cossitt, determined to secure payment of the college's debt to him, took legal action against the institution. Cossitt turned the debt of two years back wages over to the Caldwell County Sheriff's Office for collection. This action insured that his account would be the first settled. In order to settle this debt, the association issued bonds bearing ten percent interest. However, it seems unlikely that all, or even very much, of the debt to Cossitt was paid at this time.[116]

Despite his financial situation, 1839 must have had at least a few bright points for Cossitt. Middlebury College awarded him the degree Doctor of Divinity in that year. The Trustees of Cumberland College emulated this. A few months later, in March, 1840, Cossitt began publication of his **Banner of Peace** in Princeton. This periodical began as a monthly magazine but soon became a small weekly. The **Banner of Peace** allowed Cossitt a regular denomination-wide platform for his views which he continued through 1849.[117]

In 1840, Cumberland College Association considered transferring control of the college to another denomination. There is no record of how seriously this was considered. General rumor, aided by the presence of Mr. Payne on campus, had it that the college would fall into the hands of the Episcopal church. A stir was generated in the Cumberland Presbyterian Church. It was greatest, of course, in those with the closest connection to Cumberland College, Franceway Ranna Cossitt in particular. Prior to the meeting of the General Assembly in 1840, Cossitt and F. C. Usher waged a vigorous propaganda campaign in favor of keeping Cumberland College Cumberland.[118]

---

[115]Minutes of the Convention of the Cumberland Presbyterian Church, May 21-25, 1839.

[116]Evans, "Cumberland Presbyterian Colleges" 85.

[117]Beard, "Franceway Ranna Cossitt," 178, 182.

[118]Beard, "Brief Historical Sketch of Cumberland College," 156; Campbell, **Studies in Cumberland Presbyterian History**, 233.

A circular letter was widely distributed to Cumberland Presbyterian congregations. Cossitt also penned lengthy personal letters to most of the prominent ministers in the Cumberland Presbyterian Church. When it came to preserving *his* college, Cossitt resorted to every tactic. His letter to Richard Beard, dated February 3, 1840, is perhaps the first admission, in his, hand, that "we are in trouble—I have not dared to show how much." Cossitt continued,

> I have devoted the best years of my life to the College. I have done it for the Church. The Church must and will sustain it, in justice to herself, if not for me. For all that I have done, sacrificed, and suffered, I ask nothing for myself—not even thanks; but I ask that she may not suffer the fruits of her own labors, as well as mine, to go to swell the triumphs of another denomination, and to fix the indelible stain of ignorance, supineness, and covetousness upon our names and memories.

> There are forty-nine colleges and twelve theological seminaries West of the Allegheny Mountains; and I believe every one of them much better endowed than our own; yet but very few of them hold an equal standing. . . And now, my brother, shall the only Cumberland Presbyterian College pass to another denomination? The whole world would cry out 'Shame! shame!' Our very name would become a by-word and a reproach for ages to come. . . This College may die, or go into other hands, but its epitaph will be written in the everlasting disgrace of that body which founded, but did not appreciate and sustain it. . . Rely upon this fact: the more conspicuous any one may have been in founding and building up the Church, the more conspicuous must he be in the history of the loss of the College to that Church of which he was a minister. . . I can fear nothing, while faithful records are preserved. The body proposing to take the College would, I doubt not, render it a splendid Institution in a very few years. . . Believe me, if any Church under heaven needs an educated ministry, that Church is our own.[119]

Prior to the time the General Assembly met again in 1840, the

---

[119]Franceway Ranna Cossitt to Richard Beard, February 3, 1840, as recorded in Richard Beard's "Franceway Ranna Cossitt," 163-168.

position of the Cumberland College Association was nearly as bad as had been that of Barnett and the Board of Directors. The efforts of Cossitt and Usher to enlist aid for the college had made the institutions continued financial problems common knowledge in the church. Cossitt was convinced that the church would preserve Cumberland College. On April 8, 1840, he wrote Beard, "Our Church is to awake from her apathy, depend upon it." The Board of Directors of the Cumberland College Association passed a resolution to appeal to the assembly, "for aid and assistance to the college."[120]

Elkton, Kentucky, hosted the 1840 meeting of the Cumberland Presbyterian General Assembly from May 19 to 28. The business of Cumberland College first came before the delegates on Wednesday morning, May 20, when a "communication" from Finis Ewing was considered. Ewing proposed establishing an endowment for the college.[121]

Franceway R. Cossitt, Robert Donnell, John Morgan, T. C. Anderson, C. W. Fisher, W. Miller, William McGowan, and J. D. Porter were appointed to the Committee on Education which had apparently taken place of the Committee on the College. Ewing's proposal fell under their jurisdiction as did resolutions concerning the college from Vandalia and Lexington Presbyteries and the report of the report of the Cumberland College Association.[122]

The association's report reflected the consideration given to transferring control of the college to another denomination. However, it was also stated that nothing was decided nor would it be until after the meeting of the General Assembly. For their part, the association stated that they preferred to remain under the Cumberland Presbyterian denomination as long as financial support could be had from that source. Association president P. B. McGoodwin signed the

---

[120]Beard, "Brief Historical Sketch of Cumberland College," 156; Beard, "Franceway Ranna Cossitt," 168-170.

[121]Minutes of the General Assembly of the Cumberland Presbyterian Church, May 19-28, 1840.

[122]Minutes of the General Assembly of the Cumberland Presbyterian Church, May 20-21, 1840.

report on May 14, 1840.[123]

After examining the reports and testimony submitted, the Committee on Education reported that Cumberland had been profitable since the association assumed responsibility. Profits amounted to about $200 per year after operating expenses were deducted. While this was a pleasant turn, it hardly went very far toward eliminating the vast accumulated debt of the college. At the time of reporting, May 14, 1840, there were 71 students enrolled.[124]

In order to settle Cumberland College's precarious financial situation, the Committee on Education acted along the lines suggested by Finis Ewing. They recommended that the school be endowed with an adequate fund. In the minds of the committee, the association, and the General Assembly, adequate meant that enough interest would be generated to pay the salaries of the college president, faculty, and other employees as well as providing scholarships for those students preparing for ministry in the Cumberland Presbyterian Church.

> Received that this Assembly now make arrangements for the raising of a fund of $100,000 as soon as possible, the first $55,000 which when raised, shall go to endow Cumberland College, the next $30,000 to endow a college at Union Town, Fayette Co., Pa., or elsewhere within the bounds of Pennsylvania Synod, and the remaining $15,000 when collected be retained by the General Assembly or the Board, until appropriated to educational purposes.

The plan was ambitious. Still, it had the apparent support of all parties involved and gave the Cumberland Presbyterian Church the chance to show a commitment to higher education. The General

---

[123]Minutes of the General Assembly of the Cumberland Presbyterian Church, May 27, 1840.

[124]Minutes of the General Assembly of the Cumberland Presbyterian Church, May 27, 1840.

Assembly, as a whole, voted to adopt this plan.[125]

Franceway Cossitt, F. C. Fisher, J. G. Biddle, A. H. Dudley, Thomas Hunter, T. L. McNairy, William McGowan, J. H. Rackerby, F. P. McClain, A. Harpending, Robert Donnell, Finis Ewing, and John Morgan were appointed to be the new trustees of Cumberland College. Cossitt was to be president of the board, Harpending the vice president, and Rackerby the corresponding secretary. All other offices were left open but the treasurer was to be required to post bond. Once again, the Kentucky legislature was to be petitioned to alter the college charter giving these trustees control of the institution; Finis E. McLean was instructed to perform this task. On February 16, 1841, the General Assembly of the Commonwealth of Kentucky acted on the request formally transferring control of Cumberland College. The Cumberland Presbyterian General Assembly reserved the right to appoint and dismiss trustees and specified that the board should make annual reports. Satisfied with the situation, McLean commented, "The Church will be too wise ever again to part with her rights to the College."[126]

Several agents were appointed on May 28, to collect funds for the endowment. These included John L. Dillard in Middle Tennessee Synod, Reuben Burrow in West Tennessee and Columbia Synods, Finis Ewing in Missouri and Arkansas Synods, John Morgan in Pennsylvania Synod, and Joel Knight in Sangamon and Illinois Synods. Agents for the remaining synods were left to the directors

---

[125]Minutes of the General Assembly of the Cumberland Presbyterian Church, May 27, 1840; Campbell, **Studies in Cumberland Presbyterian History**, 233; Beard, "Brief Historical Sketch of Cumberland College," 157; Evans, "Cumberland Presbyterian Colleges," 96.

[126]Minutes of the General Assembly of the Cumberland Presbyterian Church, May 27, 1840; "An Act to Amend an Act, Entitled, An Act to Amend the Charter of Cumberland College, and for other Purposes," Acts of the Legislature of the Commonwealth of Kentucky, relating to Incorporating Cumberland College of Princeton, Kentucky, February 16, 1841; Evans, "Cumberland Presbyterian Colleges," 96-97; Finis E. McLean, "Cumberland College," **The Union Evangelist**, I (March 11, 1841), 1.

elect to appoint.[127]

Cossitt was sure that this plan would save Cumberland College. Writing to Beard on March 27, 1841, he stated, "the College will be endowed. We cannot doubt it. You must give up your incredulity—you will be compelled to yield it." Cossitt found that the work of trying to save the college was greater than that of administering and teaching in it. Matilda Edwards Cossitt, however, stated that "mental efforts" agreed with her husband's health. Other friends of Cossitt said that he fattened on the effort.[128]

By 1841, when the General Assembly met in Owensboro, Kentucky, it seemed that, perhaps, Cossitt's faith was justified. Reuben Burrow, S. J. Guthrie, Robert Donnell, Franceway Cossitt, and David Miller served as the Committee on Education and reported that Finis E. McLean had been successful in his petition to the General Assembly of the Commonwealth of Kentucky. Cumberland College's charter had been altered to reflect the church's wishes.[129]

The committee reported that the college was, with 75 students enrolled, in "a prosperous condition." This meant that income, amounting to $6,735.09, was equal to the year's expenses. Despite the failure of most of the agents appointed to collect for the endowment to report, it was revealed that $15,718. in cash, cash notes, and subscriptions had been collected or pledged. A further $1,333. in land had also been pledged. The Committee on Education was of the opinion that once additional agents reported, there were 24 in all, these endowment funds would increase greatly.[130]

1841 marked a radical departure from the original plan of Cumberland College as a manual labor institution. The Committee on

---

[127]Minutes of the General Assembly of the Cumberland Presbyterian Church, May 28, 1840.

[128]Franceway R. Cossitt to Richard Beard, April 8, 1840, March 27, 1841, as recorded in Richard Beard's "Franceway Ranna Cossitt," 169-71.

[129]Minutes of the General Assembly of the Cumberland Presbyterian Church, May 19, 22, 24, 1841.

[130]Minutes of the General Assembly of the Cumberland Presbyterian Church, May 19, 22, 24, 1841; Evans, "Cumberland Presbyterian Colleges," 99.

Education reported that the farm was "highly prosperous." There were about 400 acres under cultivation. Of these, 125 acres were planted in corn, 100 acres in the grains, wheat, rye, or oats, 90 acres in clover or grasses, and four acres as a vegetable garden. The college orchard also accounted for about 20 acres. Because a number of complaints had been received about the boarding institution, the board passed a resolution allowing students, with parental permission, to board off-campus. These students were to also be exempted from the two-hour labor requirement. Despite the apparent success of the farm, students were to be allowed to pay an additional fee rather than labor on the farm.[131]

Cumberland College's illusion of prosperity did not last for long. During the year following the 1841 meeting of the General Assembly of the Cumberland Presbyterian Church, Cumberland College slipped deeper and deeper into debt. By the autumn of 1841, the Cumberland College Association owed Franceway Cossitt $2,970, about four years salary. John Kendrick, the farm manager, was owed $3,070 toward his stipend.[132]

When the 1842 assembly met in Owensboro, Cumberland College's property was in danger of being auctioned by the Caldwell County sheriff in order to settle the institution's debts. The Assembly appointed Franceway Cossitt, M. B. Feemster, William Ralston, Samuel M. Aston, Samuel Bond, John McKinney, and B. Leavell to be the Committee on Education.[133]

According to a report from the Board of Trustees of the General Assembly of the Cumberland Presbyterian Church, the endowment for Cumberland College seemed to be progressing well. According to the report, made by Franceway Cossitt on May 18,

---

[131]Minutes of the General Assembly of the Cumberland Presbyterian Church, May 24, 1841.

[132]Evans, "Cumberland Presbyterian Colleges," 85; Beard, "Brief Historical Sketch of Cumberland College," 158.

[133]Evans, "Cumberland Presbyterian Colleges," 85; Beard, "Brief Historical Sketch of Cumberland College," 158; Beard, "Franceway Ranna Cossitt," 172; Minutes of the General Assembly of the Cumberland Presbyterian Church, May 18, 1842.

1842, of the 24 agents commissioned, sixteen made no report and unofficial reports were received from two. The amount officially and unofficially reported was $9,810.50 in promissory notes, and $442.63 in cash. Scholarships amounting to $5,413.33 and legacies amounting to $2,700 were also established. The total amount given or pledged was $18,366.45, an impressive total. The report was more telling, however, when it stated that the actual amount, in cash, given over to benefit the college was $447.13 toward the endowment and $345 as permanent funds. After presenting this report, Cossitt was excused from the rest of the assembly due to "feeble health."[134]

In general, the financial state of Cumberland College was not known until the Committee on Education presented a report on the afternoon of May 20, 1842. However, a memorial from Lebanon, Tennessee, was read and referred to committee on May 19, 1842, hinting that word of the institution's predicament was abroad in the church.[135]

A portion of the Committee on Education's report is worth reproducing here,

> . . .there exists a debt against the Institution of $5,654.50, which will have to be raised, or else the College property will have to be sold by process of law. . .if $2,400 were raised from resources, other than what they now possess, one thousand of which to be paid immediately, and the balance in a short time, the College could be kept in operation, otherwise not. But inasmuch as the Assembly has never agreed, or made any arrangement to raise funds to pay old debts, your Committee think it inexpedient to make any attempt to raise the amount requested. Your Committee are of opinion that it is of great importance to sustain education and literary Institutions, and in order to sustain the College and keep it in successful operation, recommend its removal to some eligible

---

[134]Minutes of the General Assembly of the Cumberland Presbyterian Church, May 18-19, 1842.

[135]Minutes of the General Assembly of the Cumberland Presbyterian Church, May 19-21, 1842.

point, so that its location will best secure that object.[136]

Perhaps the memorial from Lebanon, Tennessee, suggested the removal of Cumberland College. In the belief that there would be offers made from other locations for the relocation of the college, the Committee on Education recommended the appointment of a commission consisting of Col. Robert M. Burton, and William L. Martin his alternate, Col. George Williamson and Col. Joseph Kirkpatrick his alternate, Robert Donnell and T. C. Anderson, his alternate, Reuben Burrow and John Ralston, his alternate, Finis E. McLean, and Silas N. Davis his alternate, M. B. Feemster and James H. McReynolds, his alternate, Franceway R. Cossitt and C. G. McPherson his alternate, Col. Moses Ridley and Jacob Donaldson, his alternate, and William Ralston and C. P. Reed his alternate, to receive such propositions. Princeton, Kentucky, would be allowed to present a case for retaining the college. However, the commission was instructed to procure buildings for the use of the college until permanent buildings could be erected. So, it seemed the existence of Cumberland College in Princeton was doomed.[137]

This report sparked a great deal of debate, almost two full days. The delegates from Cumberland College Association, C. G. McPherson and F. C. Usher, were invited to take part in the debate as was Finis E. McLean, who had so recently secured alteration of the institution's charter from the Kentucky General Assembly. The delegation from Lebanon was also allowed to take part. By the end of debate, however, nothing had changed. The commission was to meet in Nashville on July 1, 1842, and entertain bids for relocating Cumberland College.[138]

---

[136]Minutes of the General Assembly of the Cumberland Presbyterian Church, May 23, 1842.

[137]Minutes of the General Assembly of the Cumberland Presbyterian Church, May 23, 1842; Minutes of the Commission to Relocate Cumberland College, February 27, 1843, as recorded in **Banner of Peace and Cumberland Presbyterian Advocate** 2 (March 10, 1843), 2.

[138]Minutes of the General Assembly of the Cumberland Presbyterian Church, May 20-21, 23, 1842; Beard, "Franceway Ranna Cossitt," 173.

RELOCATION

The commission meeting dictated by the 1842 Assembly took place in Nashville as scheduled. Bids were entertained for Cumberland College's relocation and Lebanon, Wilson County, Tennessee, emerged victorious. The Lebanon bid consisted of $10,000 in cash for the erection of a new college building as well as credible promises of support from prominent members of that community. Clearly, this support was much more concrete than that promised by Princeton had ever been. Franceway R. Cossitt was offered and accepted the presidency of the college which he held until the fall of 1844. Cornelius G. McPherson became Lebanon's first professor of the department of Mathematics and Natural Philosophy. He remained there until 1844, when he resigned. T. C. Anderson also came from Princeton's faculty to Lebanon.[139]

The Cumberland Presbyterian General Assembly's relationship with Cumberland College terminated with the end of the 1842 spring term as did Franceway Cossitt's presidency. Although the traditional founding of the school in Lebanon is July 1, 1842, Cornelius McPherson actually opened the college in September of 1842 with 45 students. President Cossitt did not arrive until February, 1843, when the second term began. Lebanon's first class graduated from Cumberland College because Tennessee did not issue a charter for Cumberland University until December 30, 1843.[140]

However, the question remains of whether Cumberland College moved from Princeton, Kentucky, to Lebanon, Tennessee, or

---

[139]Beard, "Brief Historical Sketch of Cumberland College," 157; Frank Burns, **Wilson County**, Tennessee County History Series (Memphis, Tennessee, 1983), 33-34; Beard, "Franceway Ranna Cossitt," 172-73; Howard and Hubbert, "Cumberland Presbyterian Church," 473; Minutes of the Commission to Relocate Cumberland College, February 27, 1843, and March 1, 1848, as recorded in **Banner of Peace and Cumberland Presbyterian Advocate** 2 (March 10, 1843), 2-3.

[140]Campbell, **Studies in Cumberland Presbyterian History**, 234; Burns, **Wilson County**, 33-34; Beard, "Franceway Ranna Cossitt," 173.

if the latter institution was a completely new one. Clearly, from the records of the General Assembly, the intention of the delegates and the Committee on Education was to relocate the official Cumberland Presbyterian College. References to the relocation or *removal* of Cumberland College are frequent. It is also true that the majority of the faculty of Princeton's Cumberland College and the president did relocate to the school in Lebanon. Further, the first graduating class in Lebanon, that of 1843, received degrees from Cumberland College not Cumberland University. Despite general opinion, the desires of the people involved, and the implied reality of the relocation, the simple legality of the situation speaks otherwise. Cumberland College's charter, granted by the Legislature of the Commonwealth of Kentucky, provided for the dissolution of the college and the sale of the property if it ceased to operate in Caldwell County. The Kentucky General Assembly clearly did not intend the college to move out of the county, never mind out of state. The situation is further clouded by the fact that Princeton's Cumberland College did not cease to function in 1842. The Commission to Relocate Cumberland College stated, in its minutes of March 1, 1843, that they did not have the authority to actually move Princeton's operation; however, they did have control over what school would benefit from the General Assembly's proposed educational endowment. Without doubt however, Cumberland College in Princeton was the spiritual and intellectual parent of Cumberland University in Lebanon.[141]

---

[141]Minutes of the Commission to Relocate Cumberland College, February 27, 1843, and March 1, 1843, as recorded in **Banner of Peace and Cumberland Presbyterian Advocate** 2 (March 10, 1843), 2-3.

PRINCETON FIGHTS BACK

Supporters of Cumberland College in Princeton denied that the General Assembly of the Cumberland Presbyterian Church had the authority to close the connection to the school. They maintained that, even after the establishment of the Lebanon institution, the legal connection between the assembly and Princeton school still existed. The assembly, however, decided against them.[142]

In an attempt to eliminate the Princeton school's debt and to perhaps save it, Cumberland College Association sold the farm, permanently ending the manual labor institution which B. W. McDonnold described as "a good riddance." As much property, farm equipment for example, as was possible was also liquidated. The result of these sales was that Cumberland College in Princeton was finally relieved from debt in 1842. The ten acres remaining included the college buildings, the spring, and the log building that had housed the original college. Friends of the Princeton institution rallied to its support but not in time to prevent the removal of the General Assembly's support.[143]

Despite this, the supporters of Cumberland College decided to attempt to continue the institution even without the support of the General Assembly. After all, this support had not amounted to a great deal. In 1842, clear of all but minor debts, Princeton's Cumberland College was in the best financial condition of its existence. The faculty, however, had been stripped away to Lebanon with a single exception, F. C. Usher.[144]

The *removal* of Cumberland College from Princeton spawned

---

[142]McDonnold, **History of the Cumberland Presbyterian Church**, 221.

[143]Evans, "Cumberland Presbyterian Colleges," 85; Beard, "Brief Historical Sketch of Cumberland College," 158; Campbell, **Studies in Cumberland Presbyterian History**, 234; McDonnold, **History of the Cumberland Presbyterian Church**, 226.

[144]Beard, "Brief Historical Sketch of Cumberland College,", 158-59.

a great deal of debate and animosity within the Cumberland Presbyterian Church. Sides were quickly drawn between the supporters of Princeton and those of Lebanon. Each group found a voice through newspapers published within the church. As early as 1833, in the pages of his **Cumberland Presbyterian**, Rev. James Smith expressed his displeasure with the college in Princeton and, in 1839, visited Lebanon with the intention of inspiring foundation of a church college there. Smith's animosity toward the institution seems to have originated with the tribute of ten cents per subscription that the Assembly required he give to the college. His ill feelings continued even after John Barnett voluntarily released Smith's publication from this agreement. Remarkably, after the General Assembly withdrew support from the Princeton institution, Smith shifted his support to the school, perhaps indicating that his true ire was directed toward the Assembly, not the college.[145]

The supporters of Princeton as the college's location were championed by editor Milton Bird in the pages of Uniontown, Pennsylvania's, **Union Evangelist**, while Lebanon found support, hardly surprisingly, in editor Franceway Ranna Cossitt's **Banner of Peace and Cumberland Presbyterian Advocate**.[146] On April 21, 1843, a writer signing himself only as Cumberland but probably actually Franceway Cossitt, began a series of articles defending Lebanon as a location for the college.

This article stressed the importance of ministerial education and highlights what the author considers to have been the three major problems with Cumberland College (Princeton); no "competent endowment" was secured for the college, subscriptions for support were allowed to be paid in property the value of which often proved to be inflated, and no provision was made for the instruction of probationers for the ministry free of charge. While the latter carries little weight, the former two problems certainly had effects on Cumberland College. The writer went so far as to claim that

---

[145]McDonnold, **History of the Cumberland Presbyterian Church**, 237,239-40.

[146]**Banner of Peace and Cumberland Presbyterian Advocate**, 2 (April 14, 1843), 3.

Princeton and the population of the area committed fraud. "By means of that fraud, Princeton obtained the location of the College." The author claims that the property pledged to the support of the college was overvalued and was never really worth the $28,000 often placed on it. "The failure to realize the Princeton subscription, entailed a train of evils upon the College and the church." Dealing with endowments, Cumberland claims that about $49,000 was raised or pledged at various times for the college at Princeton and that this amount would have been enough to permanently endow the institution.[147]

In the May 5, 1843, issue of the **Banner of Peace**, T. C. Anderson's article "The College Question" clearly details the extent of the animosity between the camps and their respective publications. Anderson states, "I must be permitted to express my surprise at much that has been published in the **Evangelist**, calculated to cast odium upon the trustees and friends of Lebanon College," and quotes the following attributed to Milton Bird,

> Your policy is to have the Lebanon Institution the institution of the church. Think you brethren will submit, must your College and your influence be paramount? Fasten on the church Lebanon College and perpetuate that system of operation which has for years been productive of so much evil. Its friends are making attempt *in any way* to append it to the Assembly. Think you if the Assembly find the band by which she was induced to a policy so disastrous is broken, she will stoop to allow you again to wreathe around her neck a yoke which already has proved so galling? It is madness to expect it. Settle your difficulties with the College at Princeton among yourselves. Declare in your **Banner** that a *peaceful divorce*

---

[147]Cumberland [Franceway Ranna Cossitt, probable], "Cumberland Policy," **Banner of Peace and Cumberland Presbyterian Advocate** 2 (April 21, 1843), 2; Cumberland, "Cumberland Policy.—No. 2," **Banner of Peace and Cumberland Presbyterian Advocate** 2 (April 28, 1843), 2.; Cumberland, "Cumberland Policy.—No. 3," **Banner of Peace and Cumberland Presbyterian Advocate** 2 (May 5, 1843), 2; Cumberland, "Cumberland Policy.—No. 4," **Banner of Peace and Cumberland Presbyterian Advocate** 2 (May 12, 1843), 2; Cumberland, "Cumberland Policy.—No. 5," **Banner of Peace and Cumberland Presbyterian Advocate** 2 (June 2, 1843), 2.

from the Assembly has been effected. Then we will cordially hold out the olive branch of peace and give you the embrace of brotherly love.

As an employee of Cumberland College (Lebanon), it is hardly surprising that Anderson supports that institution wholeheartedly. Despite debate and seemingly irreconcilable differences, Cumberland College (Lebanon) did prove to be permanent, as Cossitt claimed it would and gained the endowment proposed by the General Assembly for Cumberland College.[148]

There were seven graduates of Cumberland College between 1839 and the withdrawal of the General Assembly's support in 1842. Unfortunately, records of who graduated in which year have been lost. These seven were Isaac W. Taylor, L. M. Flournoy, John M. MacPherson, W. E. Warfield, John H. Phelps, H. S. Porter, and S. G. Burney.[149]

---

[148]T. C. Anderson, "The College Question," **Banner of Peace and Cumberland Presbyterian Advocate** 2 (May 5, 1843), 3-4; Franceway Ranna Cossitt, "Permanency of the College," **Banner of Peace and Cumberland Presbyterian Advocate** 2 (April 14, 1843) 3; Minutes of Columbia Synod of the Cumberland Presbyterian Church, November 4, 1842, recorded in N. P. Modrall, **Banner of Peace and Cumberland Presbyterian Advocate** 2 (March 10, 1843), 3.

[149]Beard, "Brief Historical Sketch of Cumberland College," 172.

RICHARD BEARD

Richard Beard

In 1843, the trustees offered the presidency of Cumberland College to Richard Beard, a graduate of the class of 1832. Beard accepted and on October 1, 1843, arrived to take charge. There he found F. C. Usher in place as professor of languages but J. G. Biddle, who Beard had been promised would be professor of mathematics and natural philosophy, had taken a position as a teacher in an area girl's school.[150]

Beard recorded his renewed impressions of Cumberland College,

> There were seventeen students on the ground. The brick row . . . was in ruins. The college bell was broken in pieces. There had been a great deal of recklessness and confusion connected with the closing up of the preceding year. Some of the old students had seemed to be ambitious to leave their *foot-prints* behind them. We had room enough, however, for the seventeen, and the few accessions which the new order of things brought in; and we did not need a bell for so small a number.[151]

Argument over the status of Cumberland College was raised

---

[150]**Ibid.**, 159.

[151]**Ibid.**, 159.

during the meeting of the General Assembly of 1843. The matter was hotly debated and feelings were so strong that the prospect of compromise seemed unlikely. The committee on education, in fact, was split in its opinion. Richard Beard, the committee's chair, disagreed strongly with the report that was eventually presented denouncing the connection to Princeton's Cumberland College. A protest was entered into the assembly's minutes claiming that the assembly had not handled the situation of Cumberland College in the best manner. This protest was signed by Robert Sloan, Caleb Weeden, Elam McCord, James Smith, William Henry, G. A. Fleming, Joel Lambert, F. C. Usher, David Negly, H. McDaniel, A. H. Dudley, Richard Beard, Milton Bird, James Ritchey, William Halsell, James Ashmore, A. Shelby, and P. G. Rea. An additional protest was filed by John S. Sawyer.[152]

The general bungling of financial matters concerning Cumberland prompted a resolution from the friends of the Princeton institution that stated,

> *Resolved,* That it would be unwise, impolitic, inexpedient, and contrary to the genius of presbyterian government for the General Assembly to enter into connections of a pecuniary nature giving it the supervision of any literary institution or newspaper, or otherwise to become embarrassed by the control of pecuniary matters, so as to give occasion for its moral integrity and good faith to be called in question.

Supporters of the Lebanon institution, in the main, also backed this resolution which passed with only six negative votes.[153]

At the fall meeting of Green River Synod in Hopkinsville, Kentucky, in October 1844, a suggestion was made to the synod that it might take the place of the General Assembly as sponsor of

---

[152]Minutes of the General Assembly of the Cumberland Presbyterian Church, May 16-23, 1843; McDonnold, **History of the Cumberland Presbyterian Church**, 223.

[153]Minutes of the General Assembly of the Cumberland Presbyterian Church, May 23, 1843; McDonnold, **History of the Cumberland Presbyterian Church**, 223.

Cumberland College. Despite the tentative nature of the suggestion, the synod readily agreed and offered its support to the college. Later, in the winter of the year, the same proposal was made to the Cumberland College Association which also accepted.[154]

1845 saw the first graduate of Cumberland College since the General Assembly had removed its support. Philip Riley graduated and returned to his native Mississippi. Shortly, however, Riley returned to Cumberland as professor of Languages. His return probably followed the resignation of F. C. Usher who severed his connection with Cumberland College in 1846 and accepted the position of principal for Bethel, a Cumberland Presbyterian school then located in McLemoresville, Tennessee. Riley eventually followed F. C. Usher to Bethel College, where he continued to teach as a professor of languages.[155]

Also, in 1845 or 1846, with enrollment reaching 67 students, Cumberland College was secure enough to erect a new brick building with two class rooms and four dormitory rooms. This building was constructed chiefly from material reclaimed from the wreckage of the old brick row and cost $2,600 to build. The money for the new building was raised in the Princeton area, a radical departure from the college's past. In about 1849, an additional story was added to the main college building at a cost of $4,000. Again, the funds were raised in the Princeton area.[156]

Cumberland College graduated no students in 1846. However, in 1847, 1848, and 1849, there were three graduates each year. The class of 1847 consisted of W. S. Delany, E. C. Trimble, and J. D. McGoodwin. 1848's graduating seniors were A. B. Johnson, Benjamin Shropshire, and A. J. Baird. In 1849, William B. Lambert, R. B. Lambert, and B. W. McDonnold graduated. Delany and Johnson were both the sons of early Cumberland Presbyterian ministers and both eventually entered the legal profession in

_____

[154]Campbell, **Studies in Cumberland Presbyterian History**, 234; Beard, ""Brief Historical Sketch of Cumberland College," 160.

[155]Beard, "Brief Historical Sketch of Cumberland College," 155, 160.

[156]**Ibid.**, 161-62; "Cumberland College," **Banner of Peace** (August 21, 1846), 2.

Kentucky. Both settled in Texas. A. J. Baird, William B. Lambert, and B. W. McDonnold all entered the Cumberland Presbyterian ministry.[157]

W. S. Delany, after his graduation in 1847 was employed as professor of mathematics and natural philosophy. He also later served Cumberland College as professor of languages. The post of professor of mathematics and natural philosophy was also held by Azel Freeman until his resignation in 1853. Freeman later served Bethel College and Lincoln University. Also of interest was the attempt in 1850, by the General Assembly to regain some measure of control over Cumberland College by offering to take back the responsibility that had been assumed by Green River Synod. The offer was understandably ignored.[158]

B. F. Bailey's student diary provides a rare glimpse of life at Cumberland College in 1850. About 19 years old at the time of the writing, Bailey paints a picture of the college that is some ways familiar but in others entirely alien to a modern college experience. He frequently woke before dawn, bathed, and then enjoyed frequent walks to Princeton where he often shopped or was involved in some business or another. Bailey's experience tends to minimize the supposed isolation of the college from the town.[159]

Bailey was a member of Cumberland College's Erodelphian Society and society meetings occupied a great deal of his social life. College literary societies in American higher education were the precursors of college fraternities and sororities. Bailey attended preaching regularly which, he said, was a common practice at the college. Lectures outside of the curriculum also provided entertainment. Bailey and his fellow students were particularly amused when on October 30, 1850, the speaker giving a temperance

---

[157]Beard, "Brief Historical Sketch of Cumberland College," 161-62.

[158]**Ibid.**; Ben M. Barrus, Milton L. Baughn, and Thomas H. Campbell, **A People Called Cumberland Presbyterians** (Memphis, Tennessee, 1972), 220.

[159]B. F. Bailey, [Diary], October 29 to December 5, 1850.

lecture was noticeably intoxicated.[160]

Bailey on occasion visited the ladies at "White Hall." An unnamed friend, perhaps his roommate Thomas Young, accused him of being in love with one of them, "Miss Mary E[llen]". Eventually, Bailey admitted his love for Mary Ellen to himself calling her, "an amiable and angelic creature." He vowed that his love would not overcome him and detract from his studies.[161]

Bailey marveled that few of his classmates made the effort to bathe daily nor did they often make the walk to Princeton. "I feel very much improved from daily bathing and walking. It is a strange thing to me that so few students, while cultivating their mental powers entirely neglect the improvement of their physical systems." Man was not, declared Bailey, "designed to lead the life of the sluggard."[162]

Eight men graduated as the class of 1850. They were A. G. Quaite, J. M. Quaite, J. P. Webb, J. A. McNary, A. B. George, James Vinson, W. D. Beard, and J. D. Cowen. Vinson and Cowen both entered the Cumberland Presbyterian Ministry. Vinson remained in Kentucky. J. A. McNary became a Kentucky lawyer.[163]

In 1851, six weeks before final examinations were scheduled, cholera again appeared in the vicinity of Cumberland College. Many students fled and did not return. Richard Beard claimed that there we no cases at the college.[164]

Both 1851 and 1852 saw graduating classes with six members. In 1851, T. W. Wilson, J. D. Watkins, J. W. Blue, R. D. Gwin, W. H. Miller, and J. M. Roach were granted degrees. Roach's degree, however, was honorary. In 1852, the graduates were W. C. McGehee, M. W. Baker, W. P. Nichols, B. F. Bailey, Gideon N.

---

[160] **Ibid.**, October 30-31, 1850

[161] **Ibid.**, November 23-24, 29, 1850.

[162] **Ibid.**, November 30, 1850.

[163] Beard, "Brief Historical Sketch of Cumberland College," 162.

[164] Richard Beard "Cumberland College, Princeton, Ky.," **The Cumberland Presbyterian**, 11 (August 28, 1851), 333.

Rucker, and T. H. Young. Blue and Miller both remained in Kentucky, the latter in Princeton, as lawyers. Blue served in the Kentucky Legislature. Roach and McGehee were both already ministers when they received their degrees. McGehee married a Princeton native and settled in the area.[165]

T. H. Young, after graduation in 1852, was appointed professor of natural sciences for Cumberland College. Later, he was made chair of the Department of Physical Science. The responsibility for languages was also added to Young's position after the tenure of S. P. Chesnut which lasted from 1853 to 1855.[166]

Chesnut, with W. P. Caldwell, J. H. Lowry, H. F. McNary, and A. M. McGoodwin constituted the graduating class of 1853. McNary, a Princeton native, became a physician in that town. This was the last graduating class of Cumberland College while Richard Beard was president. Early in the year Beard was offered a position in the theological department recently established at the Lebanon institution which was, by this time, Cumberland University, which he accepted. On February 13, 1854, Beard tendered his resignation as president of Cumberland College and as president of the Board of Trustees. D. W. McGoodwin replaced Beard as president of the board and by Dr. A. J. Baird as the president of Cumberland College.[167]

---

[165]Beard, "Brief Historical Sketch of Cumberland College," 162-64.

[166]Ibid., 164, 168.

[167]McDonnold, **History of the Cumberland Presbyterian Church**, 228; Beard, "Brief Historical Sketch of Cumberland College," 164-66.

DR. A. J. BAIRD & MILTON BIRD

The class of 1854, did not suffer for the change in administrations. Six men graduated; J. C. Armstrong, A. J. Patterson, G. S. Howard, A. B. Stark, E. P. Campbell, and P. H. Crider. A seventh, Cumberland Presbyterian minister, J. J. Wilson, would have graduated had he not died during the course of his senior year. Armstrong and Crider entered the ministry. Stark settled in Russellville and Patterson in Paducah.[168]

The school year that began in the fall of 1854, seemed promising to Cumberland College. The institution was still clear of debt and the number of students was recorded as "large." The faculty had grown with the addition of two new professors and the relocation of the institution closer to Princeton was considered. However, a serious disagreement seems to have developed toward the end of the year.[169]

Although the nature of the problem that developed at the end of 1854, has not been recorded, it facilitated the resignations of President Baird and Professor Chesnut. Baird resigned on January 29, 1855, and Chesnut's resignation followed shortly afterward. Azel Freeman, again serving as professor of mathematics and natural philosophy, was appointed president *pro tem*, a position he held until May 3, 1855, when Milton Bird was appointed president by the board. T. H. Young assumed Chesnut's responsibilities.[170]

According to Bird, his responsibilities as president extended only to holding the customary religious services. If this is not an exaggeration then it is unclear who was actually conducting the day-

---

[168]Beard, "Brief Historical Sketch of Cumberland College," 167.

[169]Campbell, **Studies in Cumberland Presbyterian History**, 234; Beard, "Brief Historical Sketch of Cumberland College," 167-68.

[170]Minutes of the Board of Trustees of Cumberland College, May 3, 1855, as recorded in Richard Beard's "Brief Historical Sketch of Cumberland College," 168; McDonnold, **History of the Cumberland Presbyterian Church**, 228.

to-day business of the college during Milton Bird's tenure.[171]

The class of 1855, consisted of three Cumberland Presbyterian ministers, H. D. Onyett, G. W. Kinsolving, and J. H. Nickell, and R. L. McGoodwin, who became a lawyer in Kentucky. The class of 1855, is the last for which records exist. It is likely that small graduating classes existed after this date, however.[172]

On July 9, 1855, another attempt was made to raise an endowment for Cumberland College. Perpetual and transferable scholarships were offered for sale for $100 each. These scholarships were not to be used until 300 had been sold. Interest on the $30,000 that this measure would have raised had it been successful would have been enough to support the institution. However, it seems likely that only around twenty scholarships were ever sold. By October of 1859, this endowment had generated $1,163.45 in income for Cumberland College.[173]

Before his death, John Barnett intended to donate $1,000 to Cumberland College. Perhaps this was to relieve the responsibility Barnett may have felt for the financial quagmire into which the institution slipped during the period of his management. Typical of financial matters involving Barnett, the college had difficulty in collecting. On May 18, 1857, the board recorded that they had collected $800 of the donation.[174]

---

[171]Richard Beard, "Rev. Milton Bird, D.D.," **Brief Biographical Sketches of Some of the Early Ministers of the Cumberland Presbyterian Church**, Second Series (Nashville, Tennessee, 1874), 342; Joe Ben Irby, **Life and Thought of Milton Bird, DD** (Memphis, Tennessee, 2002), 8.

[172]Beard, "Brief Historical Sketch of Cumberland College,", 168.

[173]Minutes of the Board of Trustees of Cumberland College, July 9, 1855, as recorded in Richard Beard's "Brief Historical Sketch of Cumberland College," 168-170.

[174]Minutes of the Board of Trustees of Cumberland College, May 18, 1857, as recorded in Richard Beard's "Brief Historical Sketch of Cumberland College," 169.

HAMILTON WILCOX PIERSON

Cumberland College continued in operation wholly as a Cumberland Presbyterian College until 1858. By this time, the board was experiencing great difficulty in finding faculty in the Cumberland Presbyterian Church. Competition from the growing number of Cumberland Presbyterian institutions, Bethel College in particular, made Cumberland less and less attractive.

Forced to turn outside of the Cumberland Presbyterian denomination for staff, the Board of Trustees appointed Hamilton Wilcox Pierson, a minister in the Presbyterian Church, president of Cumberland College on May 6, 1858. Hiram J. Gordon was appointed professor of languages and Thomas McCauley Ballantine professor of mathematics and natural science.[175]

Pierson was born in Bergen, New York, on September 22, 1817. He was educated at Union College and Union Theological Seminary, New York City, from which he graduated in 1848. Cumberland's trustees turned to Pierson only when no qualified applicant for the college presidency emerged from the Cumberland Presbyterian denomination. Pierson was devoted to education and to American history. Prior to his appointment to the presidency of Cumberland College, Pierson served the American Bible Society as its agent in the West Indies. There is also some indication that he was already in Kentucky at the time of his appointment. While in Kentucky he was a member of the Presbytery of Paducah.

With a president and faculty in place, the Board of Directors of Cumberland College gave the entire control of the college and the 80 students present in 1859, to the faculty for a period of ten years. They were also to have all income from tuition, board, and endowments. This measure was reported to Green River Synod, still

---

[175]Campbell, **Studies in Cumberland Presbyterian History**, 234; Minutes of the Board of Trustees of Cumberland College, May 6, 1858, as recorded in Richard Beard's "Brief Historical Sketch of Cumberland College," 169-70.

the institution's sponsoring body, at its meeting in October of 1859.[176]

By Cumberland Presbyterian tradition, the transfer of managerial control to Pierson marks the practical end of Cumberland College. Previous writings have implied that the situation at the college fell apart rapidly after Pierson was appointed president. Recently discovered documents, however, prove that it was the oncoming American Civil War that did in the college and that President Pierson and his faculty had the institution on sound financial ground.[177]

With 80 students enrolled, the 1858-1859 school year seems to have been particularly successful. M. Dudley, secretary of the trustees made a statement dated July 1, 1859, that the 1858-1859 school year had been one of "unusual prosperity" for Cumberland College. Pierson proved to be a popular choice as president. Both the religious and secular press applauded his appointment to the presidency and seemed to be equally pleased with his appointments to the faculty. Pierson's popularity resulted in a corresponding dramatic enlargement of the student body. Unfortunately, the actual size of the student body was not reported.[178]

Also, by 1859, the citizens of Princeton seem to finally have been ready to throw their much needed financial support behind the college. In order to insure that Cumberland College would be successful, they raised $20,000 for the construction of a new main building. Besides classrooms, the new building was intended to house a chapel, the library, science laboratories, and "all other necessary rooms." On July 1, 1859, the new building was reported to not only be under construction but likely to be ready for the next school year. The only indication that the new main building was ever finished comes from a letter written by Edward Thomas Broughton, a captain in the Seventh Texas Infantry, bivouacked at the site in November, 1861, during the Civil War. Broughton stated, "my quarters are in the

---

[176]Beard, "Brief Historical Sketch of Cumberland College," 170.

[177][Announcement of the faculty, terms of tuition for Cumberland College, Princeton, Ky. July 1, 1859], An American Time Capsule: Three Centuries of Broadsides and Other Printed Ephemera. Library of Congress.

[178]*Ibid.*

second story of the New Cumberland College building which is one of the finest buildings I have seen in some time."[179]

Gordon apparently lasted only one year as professor of languages. When the 1859 faculty was announced, Pierson retained his position as president and professor of mental and moral philosophy and Ballintine was still professor of mathematics and natural sciences. However Gordon was gone, replaced by Alexander Walker. Dr. James A. Carr also joined the faculty as professor of anatomy and physiology.[180]

Dudley's July 1, 1859, handbill is that last known official document related to Cumberland College. From it the structure of the institution as it stood in 1859 can be determined conclusively. The Preparatory department allowed students to finish high school before beginning their collegiate studies. Cumberland, as it had since its inception, offered the traditional "classical" course of study leading to the bachelor of arts degree. However, for the first time in 1859, a Bachelor of Science degree through a three-year course of study in the new "Scientific Department" was added. Tuition could be as little as $17 for the "common" course of study as much as $52 for the "higher" course including ancient and modern languages. All fees were expected to be paid in advance. Apparently no dormitories existed by 1859 or the college was no longer willing to employ them. Board, however, was available close to the college for $2 to $2.50 per week or "over a mile away" for $1.75 per week. The faculty consisted of President Pierson teaching mental and moral philosophy, T. McCauley Ballintine responsible for mathematics and natural sciences, Alexander Walker for Greek and Latin, and an unnamed English professor.[181]

Despite having control of the school promised to them for ten

---

[179] *Ibid.*; Edward Thomas Broughton to Mary Elizabeth Douglas Broughton, November 16, 1861, "Civil War Letters of E. T. Broughton, 7th Texas," http://battleofraymond.org/broughton.htm. Retrieved August 23, 2010.

[180] [Announcement of the faculty, terms of tuition for Cumberland College, Princeton, Ky. July 1, 1859], An American Time Capsule: Three Centuries of Broadsides and Other Printed Ephemera. Library of Congress.

[181] *Ibid.*

years, the new faculty and president only held the institution together for one more school year. The success or failure of the Cumberland class of 1860 is largely unknown. It seems certain that it was the last complete year of study that the school could manage. Given that some of the 80 students reported early in the 1859-1860 school year must have graduated, the class of 1860, must have been Cumberland College's last. Rumblings of civil unrest were growing louder and Pierson, a New England abolitionist, found himself in a particularly Confederate leaning portion of Kentucky. Although he remained in Princeton even after hostilities commenced it seems likely that he kept a very low profile. In any case, the war put an end to study at Cumberland College as it did in many other Southern institutions.[182]

From the minutes of the Board of Trustees meeting on January 8, 1861, it is revealed that President H. W. Pierson abandoned the school in June or July of 1860. The remaining school property, the library, etc., was sold to a group from Princeton who intended to operate a college in the town, presumably Princeton Collegiate Institute. Little is recorded of this enterprise and it has no connection to the Cumberland Presbyterian Church.[183]

Pierson's writings from the Civil War era indicate that he fully intended for classes to resume after the war was over. His membership remained in the Presbytery of Paducah during the entire Civil War period. While Cumberland was closed Pierson turned his attention to a biography of Thomas Jefferson which was published by Charles Scribner in 1862. Pierson was still called the President of Cumberland College at that point. At some time after finishing **Jefferson at Monticello, the Private Life of Thomas Jefferson** Pierson began teaching freedmen and African American soldiers in the Union Army. In 1862, 1863, 1864, and 1865, the minutes of the General Assembly of the Presbyterian Church indicate that Pierson was still a member of Paducah Presbytery although his physical location was in New York City in 1862-1864 and Toledo, Ohio, in

---

[182]Minutes of the Board of Trustees of Cumberland College, January 8, 1861, as recorded in Richard Beard's "Brief Historical Sketch of Cumberland College," 170-71.

[183]*Ibid.*

1865. The 1861 minutes are the last to show Pierson's residence in Princeton and the 1862 minutes are the last to indicate that he was president of Cumberland College. Pierson was described as "infirm" in 1865. The 1866 minutes of the Presbyterian Church indicate that Pierson was back in Bergen, New York.

Franceway Ranna Cossitt, the founder of Cumberland College, survived his institution for only a few years. On February 3, 1863, between four and five o'clock in the morning, Cossitt died. He had been ill for about twenty days. By 1899, B. W. McDonnold was able to say that no physical trace of Princeton's Cumberland College remained, "every vestige even of the old buildings having disappeared."[184]

McDonnold was not entirely correct. While all of the college's buildings are long decayed, the Cumberland College cemetery still exists, almost unknown, in the yard of a residential property on Traylor Street near the rear of Calvary Baptist Church in Princeton. Several markers can still be seen, none in particularly good condition, but indicating the site was still in use as late as 1868.[185] Still, within a generation or two, the physical site of Cumberland College had been all but forgotten.

As time passed, the college was romanticized almost to the point of legend. M. M. Smith, writing for the **Cumberland Presbyterian** newspaper in 1900, claimed, "the name Cumberland College arouses sacred memories in the minds of the few students now living who were educated there."[186]

The Historical committee of Kentucky Synod unveiled Kentucky historic marker number 1453 for Princeton's Cumberland College on September 24, 1972. The lawn of the Clift Rest House, then standing on the approximate site of the college buildings, hosted

---

[184]Beard, "Franceway Ranna Cossitt," 185; McDonnold, **History of the Cumberland Presbyterian Church**, 228.

[185]W. Leroy Baker to C. Ray Dobbins, December 5, 1972; "Court agrees to college park plan," *The Times Leader Online*, http://www.timesleader .net. Retrieved August 12, 2009.

[186]M. M. Smith, "The First Decade of Cumberland College," **The Cumberland Presbyterian** (February 1, 1900), 139.

the ceremony.[187]

---

[187]"Historical Marker Points to Site of Cumberland College at Princeton, Ky.," **The Cumberland Presbyterian**, 144 (November 21, 1972), 8.

The Students of Cumberland College

Unfortunately for posterity, no list of enrolled or graduating students for Cumberland College is known to have survived. The roll presented here, inaccurate as it may be, is an attempt to create such a list based on two important primary sources, the "Treasurer's Book of Cumberland College" and Richard Beard's "Brief Sketch of Cumberland College," published in the **Theological Medium** in 1876.

The "Treasurer's Book" spanning the years 1826-1848, was a manuscript record of fee payment, not a college roll. Because it recorded only cash transactions, the names of any students attending on scholarship are not included. Also, the dates recorded where those on which fees were paid which may or may not coincide with actual dates of attendance. However, given the usually strained financial situation at the college it does not seem likely that credit was extended to students for a very long period. Unfortunately, the original manuscript ledger "Treasurer's Book" has been lost. Fortunately, however, a number of years ago Mr. Sam Steger, a genealogist and local historian in Princeton, Kentucky, compiled an alphabetic typescript from the original document. Mr. Steger was obviously not familiar with the prominent Cumberland Presbyterians who attended Cumberland College during this period and some of their names are corrupted in his typescript. While this problem can be corrected for prominent individuals, it stands to reason that the names of unknown individuals were also copied incorrectly; there is no way to compensate for this.

Richard Beard, one of Cumberland College's most prominent graduates, served as the college's president from 1842 to 1853. In his history of the school, he recorded the names and dates of all of the graduates that he could remember or document. His list spans the period 1826-1855, but no specific dates are attributed to the graduates of the years 1839-1842. For these students, their dates of graduation have been assumed to be the that year in which they last appear in the Treasurer's Book. Beard recorded his history as many as fifty years after events transpired and it seems likely that his memory was not always absolutely accurate. There are slight differences between some of the names Beard records and those copied by Steger that cannot be attributed to errors in Steger's typescript. As often as possible these names have been corrected. Beard, also, seldom recorded more than just the initials of the graduates first and middle names. It is possible that other errors appear in Beard's list.

Finally, because no list of students except those graduating exists after 1848, the class rolls for 1849-1854 are an educated guess or a projection based on graduation dates and the names of students paying fees in 1848. It seems logical to assume, for example, that a student paying fees in 1848, and recorded as graduating in 1851, probably was also enrolled in 1849 and 1850. It also seems logical, since the average graduating student attended for four years, that a member of the class of 1855, for example, can be projected backward into the enrolled classes of 1852, 1853, and 1854. Obviously, with a single exception, there can be no listing or projection for students who did not graduate. After 1855, no records exist so the listings for that year must be limited to graduates and the student who is known to have died just prior to graduation.

This list does not pretend to be comprehensive or absolutely accurate. It is however, the best picture of Cumberland College's student body that can be compiled based on the sources at hand.

Some readers may complain that this list does not include a number of persons "known" to have attended the college. For this there are several reasons. Cumberland College conferred a good number of honorary degrees of various types. All persons claiming master's degrees or doctorates awarded by Cumberland can be assumed to have honorary degrees.[188] No attempt has been made to include the recipients of these honorary degrees although such a project is intriguing. The short lived Cumberland College in Nashville, Tennessee, adds an additional modicum of confusion to the situation as does Cumberland University in Lebanon, Tennessee, which graduated its first class as Cumberland College. Finally, in the days after the Civil War and long after the dissolution of Cumberland College it was possible for unscrupulous persons to claim credentials from Cumberland with little fear of contradiction. For example, Willis B. Machen, Confederate Congressman, claimed a Cumberland College degree. While it is certain that Machen attended Cumberland

---

[188]"Cumberland College," **Banner of Peace** (August 21, 1846), 2.

no documentation of his graduation can be found.[189] For these reasons only *known* and documented attendees are listed here.

Cumberland College Students
(Italics indicate graduating year)

Date of Attendance Unknown

Leonidas Austin (1826-1848)
S. G. Bradley (1826-1848)
Robert R. McKeny (1826-1848)
W. L. Sharkey (1849-1860)

1826

George Armstrong
F. E. Barnett
Robert W. Barnett
William Barnett
William H. M. Barnett
William Berry
James Blair
Alexander Brown
Malcolm Burke
A. B. Cabiness
Ewing F. Calhoun
Washington Carrol
Samuel Cumpton
William Davis
M. Dudley
William Edwards
George W. Ewing
Gilson P. Ewing
C. H. Gardner
A. C. Given
N. F. Given
Angus Grant
Ann Harpending
L. F. D. Harpending
David Harris

F. E. Harris
Joseph Hodge
Robert Hodge
W. M. Hodge
James Hutchinson
B. M. Johnson
N. C. Johnson
Fielding Jones
Henry B. Kelsoe
Henry B. King
D. Lowry
Samuel Lowry
H. Machen
H. Matchum
H. W. McClintock
James C. McCutchin
Jesse C. McCutchin
John G. McDonald
John McKeny
C. G. McPherson
John W. Ogden
John Pettus
William Rollston
Wyatt Rucker
James Ruffin
Milus Scott
Augustus Shand
Green Stewart
Thomas P. Street
John G. Thompson
Alexander Trousdale
Thomas Wadlington
James Ware
David Watts

---

[189]Berry Craig, "Caldwell native served two nations," **The Paducah Sun** (November 12, 1978), E1.

83

Cyrus W. Wilson
F. R. Wilson
Benjamin F. Young

1827

Malinda Barnett
Mary J. Barnett
P. C. Barnett
Robert W. Barnett
William H. M. Barnett
Washington Bond
Alexander Brown
Davidson Brown
William Brown
Joseph Brunston
Malcolm Burke
Virgil J. Burke
Ewing F. Calhoun
Alexander Campbell
James W. Compton
J. A. Copp
Samuel H. Craig
Thomas H. Dawson
M. Dudley
A. G. Edmondson
George W. Ewing
Gilson P. Ewing
Hamlet Ferguson
Orlando Ficklin
Wilson C. Foster
Bradford Fowler
Elijah L. Frazer
C. H. Gardner
Angus Grant
William Hamson
F. E. Harris
Russell Hewett
James Hutchinson
John W. Irwin
Neil Johnson
Fielding Jones
Henry B. Kelsoe
Henry B. King
Madison Lillard
D. Lowry

William McBride
Elam McCord
J. M. C. McCutchin
Jesse C. McCutchin
John G. McDonald
Thomas L. McNary
C. G. McPherson
Henry Metchan, Jr.
John Pettus
James W. Poage
Thomas R. Porter
J. W. Poston
Robert N. Poston
James N. Read
William H. Read
George W. Reynolds
Thomas B. Reynolds
William Rollston
Wyatt Rucker
James Ruffin
Alexander A. Scott
Milus Scott
William Shelby
John Smith
Green Stewart
Thomas P. Street
Nathan O. Terry
John G. Thompson
William Thompson
James H. Usher
Waine Wadlington
Joshua T. Walker
Robert W. Walker
William Watkins
David Watts
Edmond A. Webster
Hector R. West
Napoleon West
William Wheelock
Lewis Wilkinson
William Willard
Franklin Wilson
Elijah Woolage
William F. Wright

1828

John Allen
James M. Barbour
F. Belamy
Benjamin F. Berry
Robert M. Boggs
Washington Bond
John N. Brenton
Davidson Brown
A. Buckhannon
G. Buckhannon
J. W. Bunton
A. C. Bush
Ewing F. Calhoun
Alexander Campbell
Robert B. Castleman
James W. Compton
J. A. Copp
John L. Craig
Samuel H. Craig
Wesley Drane
A. G. Edmondson
Jordon Emery
William H. Estill
Finis Ewing
George W. Ewing
Gilson P. Ewing
Orlando Ficklin
George W. Forte
Thomas J. Forte
Wilson C. Foster
Anthony Gatewood
N. F. Given
David Harris
Cyrus Haynes
Joseph N. Hodge
Ennis D. Hurd
Henry B. Kelsoe
Henry B. King
William D. King
William Lair
D. Lowry
Matt Martin
John D. Matthews
Matthew M. Matthews
Payton P. Matthews
J. C. McCutchin

John McHenry
Thomas L. McNary
C. G. McPherson
Allen McReynolds
James T. Morris
Benjamin R. Owen
Robert A. Patterson
John D. Perryman
John Pettus
Thomas R. Porter
Robert N. Poston
Isaac B. Read
James N. Read
William H. Read
J. B. Reed
Thomas B. Reynolds
John Robertson
William P. Sappington
William Shelby
Shephard
Joseph M. Street
Thomas P. Street
Nathan O. Terry
William Thompson
F. C. Usher
A. W. Wadlington
Joshua T. Walker
Samuel W. Wardlow
William Watkins
Harvey M. Watterson
Wesley K. Watterson
Edmond A. Webster
Charles West
Benjamin F. Young
Marcus L. Young

1829

Cephus H. Andrews
John R. Angel
T. Barbee
Benjamin F. Berry
Johnathan Blair
Uriah Blue
Robert M. Boggs
Alexander Brown

85

William Brown
J. W. Bunton
Virgil J. Burke
Ewing F. Calhoun
A. G. Campbell
Robert B. Castleman
William L. Collins
Joshua Comans
Sidney Condon
J. A. Copp
John L. Craig
Silas N. Davis
William Davis
A. Delany
Wesley Drane
Rowley L. Dulin
Daniel T. Dunham
Jordon Emery
William H. Estill
William W. Famborough
J. F. Ford
George W. Forte
Thomas J. Forte
Thomas Fulks
William Garrett
Anthony Gatewood
Joseph L. George
F. Given
N. F. Given
M .H. Gleaves
John W. Goode
Bartly Gorin
Henry M. Gorin
James Gould
John F. Hall
Robert H. Hanna
William P. Harding
David Harris
John W. Harris
Cyrus Haynes
Israel L. Haynes
L. D. Haynes
Milton A. Haynes
Thomas W. Haynes
Joseph N. Hodge
W. Lacy

William Lair
Richard Lansford
James H. Lewis
Joel Lipscomb
Matt Martin
John D. Matthews
Matthew M. Matthews
Payton P. Matthews
William P. Matthews
John McBride
Joseph McBride
William McBride
Elam McCord
Jesse M. McCutchin
Samuel B. McCutchin
John McHenry
Silas H. McKay
Ferguson McKeney
Thomas L. McNary
C. G. McPherson
Allen McReynolds
A. E. Mills
John Moore
O. H. P. Moore
James T. Morris
Elias W. Napier
James L. Napier
John L. Napier
Stephen Nowlin
David D. Oldham
Benjamin R. Owen
Robert A. Patterson
John D. Perryman
James W. Poage
Thomas R. Porter
James N. Read
William H. Read
Thomas B. Reynolds
Charles W. Ridgeley
George V. Ridley
Thomas Robertson
Ewing H. Rone
John G. Rone
John Rumburgh
Sanford
William P. Sappington

Joshua P. Scott
James Searcy
George Shaw
Darwin Shelby
William Shelby
George W. Smith
Mitchell Smith
George P. Street
Thomas P. Street
Robert Temple
Nathan O. Terry
Robert L. Waddle
David L. Walker
Thomas A. Walker
Samuel W. Wardlow
Albert J. Washington
William Washington
William P. Watkins
Harvey M. Watterson
Wesley K. Watterson
Benjamin F. Weakley
Samuel D. Weakley
John C. Wear
Charles West
William West
Izekia White
Whitehead
James Wilson
Benjamin F. Young
Marcus L. Young
William C. Young

1830

William Adair
Peter Allaire
Edson Alloway
Richard H. Ball
William W. Ball
James P. Barnett
John C. Barnett
William H. M. Barnett
Richard Beard
Johnathan Blair
Samuel Blair
Robert M. Boggs

Anderson Bradley
Thomas W. Brown
C. T. Bumpass
R. W. Bumpass
A. J. M. Caldwell
Ewing F. Calhoun
Thompson Camp
L. D. Campbell
Robert B. Castleman
Joshua Comans
J. A. Copp
James L. Craig
John L. Craig
William Davis
Rowley L. Dulin
Daniel T. Dunham
Trasimond Dupuy
Mosby Edmondson
Jordon Emery
William H. Estill
William W. Famborough
Edwin G. Ford
J. F. Ford
George W. Forte
William Garrett
Anthony Gatewood
John H. Gay
D. A. Given
F. Given
G. A. Given
William Glasscock
Z. Glasscock
John W. Goode
James Gould
Thomas Green
Pleasant N. Griffin
John F. Hall
John A. Hanson
A. J. Harding
Cyrus Haynes
Milton A. Haynes
Thomas W. Haynes
Payton Hayton
Israel L. Hines
William B. Houghton
J. L. Jamerson

W. Lacy
William Lair
Edwin Lane
James H. Lewis
William P. Matthews
James G. Mayfield
Joseph McBride
William McBride
Elam McCord
J. McCutcheon
C. G. McPherson
John J. McRay
N. J. McRay
William Meade
James T. Morris
Elias W. Napier
John L. Napier
Samuel L. Napier
Peter Nicholdson
Stephen Nowlin
Robert M. Oldham
George M. Paine
John D. Perryman
James W. Poage
Thomas R. Porter
William W. Prince
James N. Read
William H. Read
C. V. Ridgeley
Charles W. Ridgeley
C. Ridgeway
George V. Ridley
Ewing H. Rone
John G. Rone
John Rumburgh
William P. Sappington
John A. Scott
John W. Scott
Darwin Shelby
George W. Smith
John G. Smith
Mitchell Smith
Sidney P. Smith
Thomas J. Smith
Sneed
David W. Sterrett

William F. Stewart
George P. Street
Thomas P. Street
Phillip L. Stump
Nathan O. Terry
W. W. Trimble
Robert L. Waddle
William Wade
David L. Walker
Thomas A. Walker
William B. Walker
Albert J. Washington
Benjamin F. Weakley
Samuel D. Weakley
John C. Wear
Charles West
Charles H. Whitaker
Hardy H. Whitaker
Madison G. Whitaker
Izekia White
Whitehead
Wilcock
William C. Woodson
Marcus L. Young
William C. Young

1831

William Adair
W. P. Alstone
Amos Anderson
Amos Andrews
Richard H. Ball
William W. Ball
William Barry
Richard Beard
Samuel Blair
Washington Bolton
Milton Bowie
Thomas W. Brown
Virgil J. Burke
Robert B. Castleman
C. Columbus
Rowley L. Dulin
Jordon Emery
William H. Estill

William W. Famborough
Edwin G. Ford
J. F. Ford
John M. Foster
John H. Gay
Joseph F. Gay
D. A. Given
G. A. Given
George W. Goza
Augustine Gradnego
Isaac Gray
Thomas Green
Pleasant N. Griffin
John A. Hanson
A. J. Harding
Thomas J. Haughton
William J. P. Haughton
Cyrus Haynes
Milton A. Haynes
Thomas W. Haynes
Abner Hester
William B. Houghton
J. L. Jamerson
H. B. Kemp
John T. Kemp
Augustus King
John E. King
John P. Koonce
Edwin Lane
Willis B. Machen
Joseph McBride
John McHenry
A. S. Mitchell
William Motley
Peter W. Ogden
George D. Oldham
Robert M. Oldham
Thomas Parker
John D. Perryman
Gustavus Phillips
Phillip Pipkin
William W. Prince
Thomas B. Reynolds
C. V. Ridgeley
Charles W. Ridgeley
Ewing H. Rone

John G. Rone
William P. Sappington
John A. Scott
William A. Scott
George W. Smith
David W. Sterrett
George P. Street
Phillip L. Stump
Stephen Treadwell
James G. Trigg
W. W. Trimble
Ralph Voorhies
Robert L. Waddle
David L. Walker
Albert J. Washington
James Watt
Hardy H. Whitaker
Madison G. Whitaker
Thomas H. Whitstone
Jones D. Wilson

1832

William Adair
W. P. Alstone
Richard H. Ball
William W. Ball
William Barnett
Richard Beard
Elijah Boggs
Achilles Collins
George M. Compton
John Darden
Stephen Darden
B. G. Dudley
Stephen Dupuy
James Edgar
Jordon Emery
William H. Estill
William W. Famborough
Edwin G. Ford
J. F. Ford
D. A. Given
Thomas J. Grace
Augustine Gradnego
Isaac Gray

89

William Gregory
Pleasant N. Griffin
Stephen F. Hale
John A. Hanson
A. J. Harding
Thomas J. Haughton
William J. P. Haughton
Cyrus Haynes
Abner Hester
William B. Houghton
Pleasant J. Hunter
Joseph Jackson
H. B. Kemp
Augustus King
John E. King
John P. Koonce
Henry R. Latimer
Willis B. Machen
Francis A. Maury
John Maxwell
Joseph McBride
A. S. Mitchell
Mark Mitchell
William Motley
Peter W. Ogden
Robert T. Ogden
George D. Oldham
Thomas Parker
Edward T. Phillips
Gustavus Phillips
Phillip Pipkin
Charles W. Ridgeley
William C. Robb
John Robertson (Robinson?)
William A. Scott
George W. Smith
John G. Smith
John Stewart
Edward Tarrent
R. D. Taylor
Stephen Treadwell
James G. Trigg
W. W. Trimble
Robert L. Waddle
Albert J. Washington
James Watt

Telemachus Weir
Madison G. Whitaker
W. H. Whitstone
James Winchester

1833

Richard H. Ball
John Biddle
Elijah Boggs
Horace Booth
James Brown
Joseph M. Brown
William R. Brown
Daniel Chapman
John L. Cocke
John Darden
Stephen Darden
B. G. Dudley
Thomas G. Duke
Stephen Dupuy
Charles Edwards
Hugh Edwards
John C. Enders
Peter Enders
J. F. Ford
R. A. Foster
Dexter P. Gordon
Pleasant N. Griffin
Stephen F. Hale
John A. Harmon
Thomas J. Haughton
William J. P. Haughton
Cyrus Haynes
Arthur Henderson
Abner Hester
Andrew Jackson, Jr.
Joseph Jackson
John P. Koonce
Theophilus Lashipelle
  (La Chapelle)
Warren Marmaduke
John Maxwell
A. S. Mitchell
Josiah B. Moore
Robert T. Ogden

George D. Oldham
Thomas Parker
John W. Pearce
Phillip Pipkin
James L. Roberts
John G. Rone
William A. Scott
A. Sharky
George W. Smith
W. B. Stewart
George P. Street
R. D. Taylor
William Taylor
James G. Trigg
Lawrence N. Waddill
Robert L Waddle
Albert J. Washington
Telemachus Weir
John Williamson
Jones D. Wilson
James Winchester

1834

William Adair
William T. Bayless
Rutledge Berry
Elijah Boggs
Thomas P. Boon
Horace Booth
Cardwell Breathitt
George Buckner
Wade H. Cathcart
Edward A. R. Cocke
John L. Cocke
George M. Compton
John Cown
John R. Denton
John Dodd
James M. C. Donnell
B. G. Dudley
Stephen Dupuy
Charles Edwards
Hugh Edwards
Peter Enders
Daniel M. Evans

James Evans
S. A. Ford
Pleasant N. Griffin
Stephen F. Hale
John A. Hanson
Thomas J. Haughton
William J. P. Haughton
Daniel M. Heard
Arthur Henderson
Abner Hester
B. M. Hughs
Joseph Jackson
O. B. Jacobs
Milton King
R. M. King
H. A. Kirkpatrick
John C. Kirkpatrick
William A. Kirkpatrick
F. Machen
John Maxwell
William H. Meredith
John M. Metcalf
George D. Oldham
James E. Pierpont
Phillip Pipkin
Joseph B. Read
Vincent Read
George B. Ridley
William C. Robb
James L. Roberts
James M. Smith
W. B. Stewart
A. Talkington
James G. Taylor
Joseph W. Taylor
R. D. Taylor
William Taylor
James Terry
B. W. Thompson
James G. Trigg
Oscar Ward
Albert J. Washington
Allen Watson
George L. Watson
Samuel Watson
W. L. Watson

J. F. Z. Whitesides
Thomas H. Whitstone
James T. Young
William L. Young

1835

Joseph Carter
Wade H. Cathcart
James B. Cherry
Henry Crutcher
Joel E. Davis
Samuel W. Davis
Phillip T. Day
Samuel C. Debour
John R. Denton
James M. C. Donnell
B. G. Dudley
Charles Edwards
Hugh Edwards
Peter Enders
S. A. Ford
R. A. Foster
C. C. Frazer
W. R. Frazer
Robert E. Frius
James T. Garnett
E. F. Grinstead
Stephen F. Hale
John A. Hanson
Thomas J. Haughton
William J. P. Haughton
James D. Heady
Daniel M. Heard
M. J. Horn
T. J. Houghton
William J. Houghton
Jasper Ingram
Robert Ingram
Felix Johnson
R. M. King
H. A. Kirkpatrick
John C. Kirkpatrick
William A. Kirkpatrick
Theophilus Lashipelle
    (La Chapelle)

F. Machen
Edward A. Martin
Joseph B. Martin
Thomas J. McCormick
J. W. L. McDonald
P. M. McDonald
George McDuffy
Malcolm McInnis
John M. Metcalf
John B. Miller
John T. Molloy
M. B. Molloy
William Norris
John Patrick
W. M. D. Pendergast
W. R. Peobles
E. V. H. Perkins
William J. Perkins
Phillip Pipkin
Joseph B. Read
Robert J. Reeves
George B. Ridley
John L. Roane
James L. Roberts
William Roberts
Joe B. Rolls
Silas M. Rolls
George A. Ross
A. Shances
N. B. Sharky
R. D. Sharky
Jackson Simpson
James G. Taylor
Joseph W. Taylor
R. D. Taylor
William Taylor
Telenichus Walker
James H. Ward
Oscar Ward
J. H. Whetstone
Benjamin W. Whitfield
Theodore Whitstone
Thomas H. Whitstone
John L. Williamson
James T. Young
William L. Young

1836

James L. Alcorn
Nathaniel V. Allen
John Baragne
W. E. Barnett
Leander Berry
William K. Blue
C. G. Borah
Franklin W. Bradley
Joseph Carter
Wade H. Cathcart
James B. Cherry
Isaac Davis
Joel E. Davis
John R. Davis
Robert A. Davis
Samuel W. Davis
John R. Denton
James M. C. Donnell
B. G. Dudley
Samuel C. Dunlap
Robert W. Edmondson
Peter Enders
H. G. Estill
Thomas R. Fitus
Lafayette Flournoy
C. C. Frazer
Jordan Fretwell
James T. Garnett
Joshua D. Grant
John P. Gray
Stephen F. Hale
M. L. Hardgrove
D. R. Harris
Thomas L. Henry
B. K. Hunter
Jasper Ingram
Robert Ingram
Felix Johnson
John C. Kirkpatrick
William A. Kirkpatrick
Theophilus Lashipelle
 (La Chapelle)
A. L. Lenoir
William P. Lewis

James Lynch
Presley Maxwell
Thomas J. McCormick
George McDuffy
John C. McLoud
John D. Meek
A. J. D. Mitchell
M. B. Molloy
William P. Nixon
A. Owen
W. M. D. Pendergast
Robert D. Ray
Robert J. Reeves
Joshua C. Reynolds
Isaac Ritchey
John K. Ritchey
John N. Roach
John L. Roane
John C. Rolls
Silas M. Rolls
Ewing H. Rone
Robert L. Ross
Isaac Shelby
James M. Smith
Washington Smith
Samuel G. Stevens
Zadock Stevens
Ayers Stewart
J. M. Taylor
James G. Taylor
Joseph W. Taylor
R. D. Taylor
William Taylor
G. W. Usher
Manuel M. Valdez
Walter Warfield
George L. Watson
Lewis A. Webb
John West
J. F. Z. Whitesides
Joshua R. Wilcox
William L. Young

1837

George Armstrong
Cuthbert Berry
Leander Berry
J. G. Biddle
John Bone
Franklin W. Bradley
Thomas Brooks
James B. Cherry
Albert D. Cosby
William A. Cothran
B. G. Dudley
Robert W. Edmondson
R. C. D. Ewing
Lafayette Flournoy
James T. Garnett
David Greer
Dickson Greer
Stephen F. Hale
M. L. Hardgrove
Preston Henley
Thomas L. Henry
J. Hopson
A. Johnson
E. S. Johnson
James E. Johnson
John E. Johnson
R. M. King
Theophilus Lashipelle
        (La Chapelle)
Henry R. Latimer
John P. M. Lewis
John H. Maddox
William McArthur
Thomas J. McCormick
Jesse McHenry
J. H. McKee
Samuel C. McNees
W. B. Miller
George D. Mitchell
W. M. D. Pendergast
John H. Phelps, Jr.
Thomas Phelps
William Phelps, Jr.
Charles Pipes

David Pipes
Thomas M. Rankin
Robert D. Ray
Oscar Ream
Robert J. Reeves
Isaac Ritchey
John N. Roach
John C. Rolls
Silas M. Rolls
Robert L. Ross
L. W. Rudisel
R. M. Rudisel
James Simpson
Washington Smith
William B. Spear
John A. Stevens
Ayers Stewart
Matthew Stoker
William Stoker
Isaac W. Taylor
Henry Trotter
Thomas Trotter
Hiram Twitchel
Jesse B. Ward
Thomas M. Ward
Walter Warfield
Lewis A. Webb
Joshua R. Wilcox
James P. Williamson
William L. Young

1838

E. Adams
Stephen G. Adams
Cuthbert Berry
Leander Berry
Robert T. Bigham
John Bone
N. H. Borah
H. M. Bradley
Willis Bradley
Thomas Brooks
S. G. Burney
James B. Cherry
John W. Chinn

Henry L. Conn
Albert D. Cosby
William A. Cothran
H. G. Estill
R. C. D. Ewing
Austin Flanakin
Lafayette Flournoy
John M. Foster
Elijah L. Frazer
James T. Garnett
John W. Goar
David Greer
H. G. Hams
Henry G. Harris
Thomas L. Henry
Gustavus Hodge
Washington Hodge
James Hunt
Charles E. Hynson
James Key
John Key
Thomas B. Lamb
Henry R. Latimer
Leftwich
Henry L. Leigh
John P. M. Lewis
James A. Lusk
John H. Maddox
Samuel G. Marshall
James B. Mason
William McArthur
D. P. McCollum
Thomas J. McCormick
B. F. McCutchin
Jesse McHenry
J. H. McKee
Samuel C. McNees
John D. Meek
W. B. Miller
H. G. Moore
Thomas Moore
G. K. N. Pendergast
W. M. D. Pendergast
John H. Phelps, Jr.
Thomas Phelps
William Phelps, Jr.

A. G. Pickard
J. H. Pickard
Charles Pipes
James W. Pritchett
W. G. L. Quaite
Thomas C. Quirk
Willis R. Ramsay
Edmond R. Ray
Robert D. Ray
Oscar Ream
John N. Roach
John R. Rochelle
John C. Rolls
Robert L. Ross
L. W. Rudisel
R. M. Rudisel
Washington Smith
Gale V. Snidicor
John A. Stevens
Isaac W. Taylor
Richard Taylor
Henry Trotter
Thomas Trotter
Thomas M. Ward
Walter Warfield
Lewis A. Webb
Naron C. Whyte
Joshua R. Wilcox
Abraham C. Yager
William L. Young

1839

Robert T. Bigham
George W. Bone
Jacob Borah
N. H. Borah
H. M. Bradley
Willis Bradley
Clark H. Brashier
John F. Brigham
William B. Brodie
Thomas Brooks
Thomas G. Burney
Anson C. Capshan
James B. Cherry

95

James A. Clark
S. C. Cowan
Thomas J. Curd
Charles Davis
R. A. Davis
Elisha Edwards
Asa M. Finley
Lafayette Flournoy
Thomas Glass
Thomas L. Hardgrove
Henry G. Harris
William Heath
Thomas Hobson
Gustavus Hodge
Washington Hodge
James Hunt
John Hunter
J. H. Husbands
A. D. Hustin
William G. Johnson
James Key
John Key
Thomas Kidd
Henry R. Latimer
Henry L. Leigh
Thomas Long
James A. Lusk
John H. Maddox
Sam S. Manhall
D. P. McCollum
B. F. McCutchin
John D. Meek
Thomas Moore
John H. Nicholds
Benjamin Petway
John H. Phelps, Jr.
Thomas Phelps
William Phelps, Jr.
A. G. Pickard
J. H. Pickard
H. S. Porter
Joseph H. Porter
Cuthbert Price
William S Price
James W. Puckett
W. G. L. Quaite

Thomas C. Quirk
Thomas M. Rankin
Edmond R. Ray
P. G. Rea
R. L. Reeves
Gale V. Snidicor
John A. Stevens
William H. Tapp
Isaac W. Taylor
John A. Throckmorton
Joseph Waddill
Otway Waddill
Martin K. Walker
Walter Warfield
Lewis A. Webb
James C. Wooldridge
Robert Wooldridge
Abraham C. Yager

1840

Stephen G. Adams
G. F. Ashford
J. B. Ashford
Robert T. Bigham
William H. Blackman
George W. Bone
Jacob Borah
Joseph T. Borah
William D. Boswell
Clark H. Brashier
John F. Brigham
C. A. Brodie
William B. Brodie
Thomas Brooks
Churchill Buck
John P. Burk
S. G. Burney
Thomas G. Burney
William Caskey
B. C. Chapman
D. W. Christian
Giles L. Cobb
J. Collins
Francis Dabney
George Dameron

Charles Davis
J. H. Davis
John T. Dawson
Plummer W. Dawson
William M. Dillard
George H. Diuquid
M. N. Diuquid
Henry Duncan
Joseph Ensley
A. B. Ewing
C. L. Ewing
E. B. Ewing
Asa M. Finley
A. F. Flournoy
Jordon Flournoy
Thomas C. Foushee
John Gilley
J. Ewing Gleaves
Alfred Going
William W. Goodwin
Samuel Gray
P. H. Grinstead
Edward P. H. Grooms
Thomas L. Hardgrove
Henry G. Harris
John W. Headley
James Hunt
James Kendrick
John H. Kendrick
James Key
John Key
Henry R. Latimar
Henry L. Leigh
Rinaldo Marble
Samuel G. Marshall
William Martin
W. W. McGraw
George D. McLean
R. F. Motherel
James L. Murphy
A. M. Newman
John H. Nicholds
Thomas G. Noel
George Park
Sylvester Parson
Robert Patton

Jacob N. Penick
Benjamin Petway
Hinchy Petway
Cuthbert Price
William S Price
James W. Puckett
John W. Puckett
Edmond R. Ray
P. G. Rea
Finnis E. Roberts
Rowland Robertson
Joel Simpson
John J. B. Slater
Launer M. Slater
Gale V. Snidicor
John Sodon
Drury C. Stevens
John E. Stevens
William Stewart
William H. Tapp
Isaac W. Taylor
John A. Throckmorton
Otway Waddill
Martin K. Walker
Walter Warfield
Noah Watkins
John M. Weakley
George C. West
Elisha Williams
B. A. Wood
James C. Wooldridge
Robert Wooldridge
B. W. Wright

1841

Stephen G. Adams
G. F. Ashford
J. B. Ashford
W. C. Blackburn
David Boswell
William D. Boswell
William Branch
William P. Bressen
John F. Brigham
Churchill Buck

James Cade
John B. Cade
Alexander Campbell
B. C. Chapman
Robert Chiles
Curtis Couch
Thomas Couch
K. W. Cunningham
Francis Dabney
John Daniel
John T. Dawson
Plummer W. Dawson
William M. Dillard
Henry Duncan
William A. East
Andrew T. Edwards
Joseph Ensley
Robert B. Erwin
Robert A. Erwine
A. B. Ewing
C. L. Ewing
E. B. Ewing
Phillip Field
Thomas C. Foushee
Lafayette Freeman
J. Ewing Gleaves
Joseph D. Glover
Alfred Going
William W. Goodwin
William Gorin
William J. Graham
Samuel Gray
Thomas L. Hardgrove
John R. Horn
Samuel Hudson
Hezekiah James
Robert T. Jarman
Thomas S. Jarman
Thomas Johns
M. A. Kerr
James Key
John Key
Henry R. Latimar
Henry L. Leigh
Charles M. Liesure
William Louth

Rinaldo Marble
Joseph Martin
Thomas Martin
William Martin
Thomas N. McKee
George D. McLean
Joseph McReynolds
Robert G. Morman
R. F. Motherel
A. M. Newman
Benjamin Petway
Hinchy Petway
William Phelps, Jr.
Peter Phillips
William Phillips
Cuthbert Price
James W. Puckett
Finnis E. Roberts
William S. Sanford
Aaron J. D. Shelby
Finis E. Shelby
John B. Shelby
Russell Shelby
William Shelby
Dudley Y. Shepherdson
James J. Sim
John A. Sim
Launer M. Slater
Wallace Smith
John Sodon
Drury C. Stevens
William H. Tapp
Thomas J. Terry
Martin K. Walker
Walter Warfield
Robert P. Waring
Daniel B. Whalen
E. A. White
J. M. White
J. O. White
Samuel J. White
Thomas J. White
Elisha Williams
S. L. Wooldridge

1842

98

Patrick Barnett
William E. Beeson
David Boswell
William D. Boswell
James G. C. Bothwell
John F. Burney
James Cade
John B. Cade
Robert Chiles
Garland Cosby
Nathan Craddock
K. W. Cunningham
A. L. Daniel
Henry Duncan
Andrew T. Edwards
John R. Edwards
William Edwards
A. B. Ewing
C. L. Ewing
E. B. Ewing
T. T. Ewing
Phillip Field
James Fowler
William J. Graham
Samuel M. Hampton
D. L. Herron
John R. Horn
Samuel Hudson
Hezekiah James
John Key
Milton Lamb
Charles M. Liesure
William Louth
John M. MacPherson
Joseph McReynolds
William F. Mitchell
Samuel Moore
W. N. Motherel
John H. Phelps, Jr.
Peter Phillips
William Phillips
Cuthbert Price
Finis E. Shelby
John B. Shelby
Russell Shelby
Dudley Y. Shepherdson

James J. Sim
John A. Sim
Martin K. Walker
Walter Warfield
Daniel B. Whalen
M. B. Winstead

1843

Stephen F. Bell
George W. Bone
Henry L. Caldwell
James H. Calvert
Pattilla Calvert
Demarkus L. Cash
James R. Ford
F. L. Fowler
John T. Gage
William J. Graham
William R. Gray
Patrick H. Halstead
Daniel Haynes
H. B. Irvan
Robert Lander
Leonard L. Leach
David A. Maxwell
James H. Maxwell
John D. McGoodwin
John D. McGowan
John W. McGowan
John D. McNahan
John A. McNary
Samuel E. McNary
William S. McNary
John E. Mercer
Junior C. Miller
R. Y. Northem
James Pearce
Nicholas Pearce
James L. Ramsay
James S. Ramsay
Phillip Riley
Finnis E. Roberts
Aaron J. D. Shelby
Russell Shelby
John C. Smith

M. M. Smith
Robert E. D. Smith
Thadeous C. Smith
John J. Wiley
D. F. Wyatt

1844

Robert E. Beard
William D. Beard
Henry L. Caldwell
Pattilla Calvert
R. M. Calvert
F. M. Cash
John T. Crayton
Jesse Daniel
William J. Duncan
Francis Ford
F. L. Fowler
John T. Gage
William J. Graham
Daniel Haynes
John L. Irwin
Burnell B. Irwine
Thomas Johns
Alfred B. Johnson
Robert B. Lambert
William R. Lambert
Thomas Love
John M. Massey
David A. Maxwell
John D. McGoodwin
J. M. McLin
Hugh McNary
John A. McNary
Samuel E. McNary
John E. Mercer
N. T. E. Mitchusson
James Pearce
Nicholas Pearce
Laban Phelps
Lafayette Phelps
John Rackerly
James L. Ramsay
James S. Ramsay
Phillip Riley

Aaron J. D. Shelby
Russell Shelby
Dudley Y. Shepherdson
L. B. Shotwell
M. M. Smith
Robert E. D. Smith
Thadeous C. Smith
John J. Wiley
M. B. Winstead

1845

George H. Ames
Robert Baker
Robert E. Beard
William D. Beard
James W. Cail
Henry L. Caldwell
Pattilla Calvert
W. S. Delany
William J. Duncan
Francis Ford
John T. Gage
William H. Gorin
William P. Grace
William J. Graham
Daniel Haynes
John L. Irwin
Alfred B. Johnson
Robert B. Lambert
William R. Lambert
Thomas Love
M. M. Lyon
David A. Maxwell
D. W. McGoodwin
Matthew W. McKinney
Daniel McKinsay
Hugh McNary
John A. McNary
Samuel E. McNary
J. F. Mitchusson
N. T. E. Mitchusson
J. T. Moore
James Pearce
Nicholas Pearce
T. W. Pretteman

John Rackerly
William C. Rackerly
James L. Ramsay
James S. Ramsay
J. H. Rayburn
Thomas J. Reeves
Phillip Riley
Gideon N. Rucker
Dudley Y. Shepherdson
L. B. Shotwell
Benjamin Shropshire
Thadeous C. Smith
N. T. Turner
John D. Tyler

1846

John Q. Allen
Robert E. Beard
William D. Beard
William Bishop
J. M. Bradford
Henry L. Caldwell
R. A. Cobb
R. A. Davidge
W. S. Delany
G. W. H. Earnas
William P. Grace
William Grove
Leland S. Head
J. A. Ingram
Richard B. Jackson
Alfred B. Johnson
J. St. Clair Kurkendall
Robert B. Lambert
William R. Lambert
C. P. Lyon
M. M. Lyon
J. P. McGoodwin
John D. McGoodwin
J. J. McKeil
Hugh McNary
John A. McNary
Samuel E. McNary
John E. Mercer
N. T. E. Mitchusson

James T. Moon
J. T. Moore
W. G. Norman
James Pearce
Nicholas Pearce
John Rackerly
J. H. Rayburn
Thomas J. Reeves
Robert Riley
Gideon N. Rucker
J. E. Satterfield
L. D. Shelby
J. B. Shell
Benjamin Shropshire
John D. Tyler
M. Walsh
James P. Webb
Thomas Young

1847

John Q. Allen
J. H. Beard
Richard Beard, Jr.
Robert E. Beard
William D. Beard
William Bishop
J. E. Blackburn
J. W. Blue
H. C. Bonner
J. M. Bradford
P. Broyles
Charles H. Brunk
Henry L. Caldwell
Charles Camel
W. S. Delany
B. F. Doris
Fleming
S. D. Hawthorne
Leland S. Head
Richard B. Jackson
Alfred B. Johnson
Robert B. Lambert
William R. Lambert
William W. Love
A. M. McGoodwin

J. P. McGoodwin
John D. McGoodwin
J. W. McKee
J. J. McKeil
Hugh McNary
John A. McNary
Samuel E. McNary
John E. Mercer
William H. Mitchell
N. T. E. Mitchusson
James T. Moon
W. E. Moore
W. G. Norman
S. A. Nunn
James Pearce
Angus Quate
Joseph M. Quate
Lafferty Quigley
Q. Q. Quigley
William C. Rackerly
J. H. Rayburn
Thomas J. Reeves
Gideon N. Rucker
J. E. Satterfield
L. D. Shelby
J. B. Shell
Benjamin Shropshire
R. C. Sloo
T. Thompson
E. C. Trimble
E. L. Varnell
W. W. Warrel
B. W. Wasson
James P. Webb
J. I. Young
J. W. B. Young
Thomas Young

1848

B. F. Baily
A. J. Baird
C. Barbour
W. G. Barbour
J. Barnett
J. H. Beard

Richard Beard, Jr.
Robert E. Beard
William D. Beard
N. H. Bigham
William Bishop
J. E. Blackburn
J. W. Blue
P. Broyles
Charles H. Brunk
Charles Camel
John Cane
W. F. Coates
W. G. Coates
W. S. Coates
J. B. Cowan
B. F. Doris
F. P. Edwards
Fleming
A. B. George
G. G. Gray
William Grove
S. D. Hawthorne
Leland S. Head
A. G. Horne
J. Hutchinson
Richard B. Jackson
Alfred B. Johnson
J. A. Kreykendall
Robert B. Lambert
A. M. McGoodwin
J. W. McKee
J. J. McKeil
Hugh McNary
John A. McNary
Samuel E. McNary
William H. Mitchell
N. T. E. Mitchusson
W. E. Moore
J. T. Morse
James T. Morse
H. S. Mullins
S. A. Nunn
L. Phelps
R. C. Phelps
Angus Quate
Joseph M. Quate

Lafferty Quigley
Q. Q. Quigley
Gideon N. Rucker
J. E. Satterfield
Benjamin Shropshire
R. C. Sloo
J. W. Smith
T. Thompson
E. L. Varnell
B. W. Wasson
J. D. Watkins
James P. Webb
A. J. Wells
F. W. Wilson
J. H. Young
J. W. B. Young

1849

B. F. Bailey
M. W. Baker
William D. Beard
J. W. Blue
J. D. Cowen
A. B. George
R. D. Gwin
Robert B. Lambert
William R. Lambert
B. W. McDonnold
W. C. McGehee
A. M. McGoodwin
John A. McNary
W. H. Miller
W. P. Nichols
A. G. Quaite
J. M. Quaite
J. M. Roach
Gideon N. Rucker
James Vinson
J. D. Watkins
James P. Webb
T. W. Wilson
T. H. Young

1850

B. F. Bailey
M. W. Baker
William D. Beard
J. W. Blue
W. P. Caldwell
S. P. Chesnut
J. D. Cowen
A. B. George
R. D. Gwin
J. H. Lowry
W. C. McGehee
A. M. McGoodwin
H. F. McNary
John A. McNary
W. H. Miller
W. P. Nichols
A. G. Quaite
J. M. Quaite
J. M. Roach
Gideon N. Rucker
James Vinson
J. D. Watkins
James P. Webb
T. W. Wilson
T. H. Young

1851

J. C. Armstrong
B. F. Bailey
M. W. Baker
J. W. Blue
W. P. Caldwell
E. P. Campbell
S. P. Chesnut
P. H. Crider
R. D. Gwin
G. S. Howard
J. H. Lowry
W. C. McGehee
A. M. McGoodwin
H. F. McNary
W. H. Miller
W. P. Nichols
A. J. Patterson
J. M. Roach

Gideon N. Rucker
A. B. Stark
J. D. Watkins
J. J. Wilson
T. W. Wilson
T. H. Young

1852

J. C. Armstrong
B. F. Bailey
M. W. Baker
W. P. Caldwell
E. P. Campbell
S. P. Chesnut
P. H. Crider
G. S. Howard
G. W. Kinsolving
J. H. Lowry
W. C. McGehee
A. M. McGoodwin
R. L. McGoodwin
H. F. McNary
W. P. Nichols
J. H. Nickell
H. D. Onyett
A. J. Patterson
Gideon N. Rucker
A. B. Stark
J. J. Wilson
T. H. Young

1853

J. C. Armstrong
W. P. Caldwell
E. P. Campbell
S. P. Chesnut
P. H. Crider
G. S. Howard
G. W. Kinsolving
J. H. Lowry
A. M. McGoodwin
R. L. McGoodwin
H. F. McNary
J. H. Nickell

H. D. Onyett
A. J. Patterson
A. B. Stark
J. J. Wilson

1854

J. C. Armstrong
E. P. Campbell
P. H. Crider
G. S. Howard
G. W. Kinsolving
R. L. McGoodwin
J. H. Nickell
H. D. Onyett
A. J. Patterson
A. B. Stark
J. J. Wilson

1855

G. W. Kinsolving
R. L. McGoodwin
J. H. Nickell
H. D. Onyett

Known Graduates of Cumberland College

Amos Andrews 1831
J. C. Armstrong 1854
B. F. Bailey 1852
A. J. Baird 1848
M. W. Baker 1852
Richard H. Ball 1833
James P. Barnett 1830
W. E. Barnett 1836
William Barnett 1832
Richard Beard 1832
William D. Beard 1850
J. G. Biddle 1837
J. W. Blue 1851
S. G. Burney 1840
W. P. Caldwell 1853
Ewing F. Calhoun 1829

Ewing F. Calhoun 1830
E. P. Campbell 1854
Robert B. Castleman 1831
S. P. Chesnut 1853
J. A. Copp 1829
J. D. Cowen 1850
P. H. Crider 1854
A. Delany 1829
W. S. Delany 1847
John R. Denton 1836
B. G. Dudley 1837
Rowley L. Dulin 1831
William H. Estill 1832
Lafayette Flournoy 1839
J. F. Ford 1833
A. B. George 1850
Pleasant N. Griffin 1834
R. D. Gwin 1851
Stephen F. Hale 1837
John A. Hanson 1834
D. R. Harris 1836
Cyrus Haynes 1833
T. J. Houghton 1835
William J. Houghton 1835
G. S. Howard 1854
Alfred B. Johnson 1848
Fielding Jones 1827
Henry B. King 1828
G. W. Kinsolving 1855
John C. Kirkpatrick 1836
Robert B. Lambert 1849
William R. Lambert 1849
J. H. Lowry 1853
John M. MacPherson 1842
J. McCutcheon 1830
B. W. McDonnold 1849
W. C. McGehee 1852
A. M. McGoodwin 1853
John D. McGoodwin 1847
R. L. McGoodwin 1855
H. F. McNary 1853
John A. McNary 1850
C. G. McPherson 1830
W. H. Miller 1851
A. S. Mitchell 1833
John Moore 1827

W. P. Nichols 1852
J. H. Nickell 1855
H. D. Onyett 1855
A. J. Patterson 1854
John H. Phelps, Jr. 1842
Thomas Phelps 1838
H. S. Porter 1839
A. G. Quaite 1850
J. M. Quaite 1850
Robert D. Ray 1838
Thomas B. Reynolds 1831
Charles W. Ridgeley 1832
Phillip Riley 1845
J. M. Roach 1851
John L. Roane 1836
Gideon N. Rucker 1852
William A. Scott 1833
Benjamin Shropshire 1848
George W. Smith 1833
A. B. Stark 1854
Isaac W. Taylor 1840
J. M. Taylor 1836
Joseph W. Taylor 1836
E. C. Trimble 1847
F. C. Usher 1828
G. W. Usher 1836
James Vinson 1850
Lawrence N. Waddill 1833
A. W. Wadlington 1828
Walter Warfield 1842
J. D. Watkins 1851
James P. Webb 1850
J. H. Whetstone 1835
T. W. Wilson 1851
T. H. Young 1852

WORKS CITED

Acts of the Legislature of the Commonwealth of Kentucky, relating to Incorporating Cumberland College of Princeton, Kentucky. January 8, 1827.

"An Act to Amend the Charter of Cumberland College, and for other Purposes." Acts of the Legislature of the Commonwealth of Kentucky, relating to Incorporating Cumberland College of Princeton, Kentucky. February 16, 1838.

"An Act to Amend an Act, Entitled, An Act to Amend the Charter of Cumberland College, and for other Purposes." Acts of the Legislature of the Commonwealth of Kentucky, relating to Incorporating Cumberland College of Princeton, Kentucky. February 16, 1841

[Announcement of the faculty, terms of tuition for Cumberland College, Princeton, Ky. July 1, 1859]. An American Time Capsule: Three Centuries of Broadsides and Other Printed Ephemera. Referenced February 20, 2007, from http://memory.loc.gov/ammem/index.html.

Bailey, B. F. [Diary], October 29, 1850, to December 5, 1850.

Baird, Nancy D. "Asiatic Cholera's First Visit to Kentucky: A Study in Panic and Fear." **Filson Club History Quarterly**, 48 (1974), 228-40.

Baker, W. Leroy, to C. Ray Dobbins. December 5, 1972.

Banner of Peace and Cumberland Presbyterian Advocate, 2 (March 10, 1843).

Barrus, Ben M., Milton L. Baughn, and Thomas H. Campbell. **A People Called Cumberland Presbyterians**. Memphis, Tennessee, 1972.

Beard, Richard "Brief Historical Sketch of Cumberland College, At Princeton, Kentucky. 1825-1861." **Theological Medium, A Cumberland Presbyterian Quarterly**, 12 (April, 1876), 129-172.

Beard, Richard. "Cumberland College, Princeton, Ky.," **The Cumberland Presbyterian**, 11 (August 28, 1851), 333.

Beard, Richard. "Franceway Ranna Cossitt, D.D. 1822-1863." **Brief Biographical Sketches of Some of the Early Ministers of the Cumberland Presbyterian Church**. Nashville, Tennessee, 1867.

Beard, Richard. "Funeral Sermon, Occasioned by the Death of Mrs. Lucinda

Cossitt, Consort of the Rev. F. R. Cossitt, President of Cumberland College, and Delivered at the Request of the Deceased. Princeton, Ky, Sabbath, March 17, 1833." **Cumberland Presbyterian Pulpit**, I (May, 1833), 65-79.

Beard, Richard. "Rev. Milton Bird, D.D." **Brief Biographical Sketches of Some of the Early Ministers of the Cumberland Presbyterian Church**. Second Series. Nashville, Tennessee, 1874.

Broughton, Edward Thomas, to Mary Elizabeth Douglas Broughton. November 16, 1861. Retrieved August 23, 2010, from http://battleofraymond.org/broughton.htm.

Burns, G. Frank. **Phoenix Rising; the Sesquicentennial History of Cumberland University, 1842-1992**. Lebanon, Tennessee, 1992.

_____. **Wilson County**. Tennessee County History Series. Memphis, Tennessee, 1983.

Campbell, Thomas H. **Good News on the Frontier**. Memphis, Tennessee, 1965.

_____. **Studies in Cumberland Presbyterian History**. Nashville, Tennessee, 1944.

"Cossitt Family Information," retrieved February 11, 2007, from http://www.cumberland.org/hfcpc/minister/Cossitt.htm.

Cossitt, Franceway Ranna, to Rodrick Horton, November 26, 1832.

Cossitt, Franceway Ranna. **The Life and Times of Rev. Finis Ewing One of the Fathers and Founders of the Cumberland Presbyterian Church, to Which is Added Remarks on Davidson's History , or, a Review of His Chapters on the Revival of 1800, and His History of the Cumberland Presbyterians**. Louisville, Kentucky, 1853.

"Court agrees to college park plan." *The Times Leader Online*, http://www.timesleader.net. Retrieved August 12, 2009.

Craig, Berry. "Caldwell native served two nations." **The Paducah Sun** (November 12, 1978), E1.

"Cumberland College." **Banner of Peace and Cumberland Presbyterian Advocate** (November 24, 1843), 2.

"Cumberland College." **Banner of Peace** (August 21, 1846), 2.

Cumberland Synod of the Cumberland Presbyterian Church (Franceway Ranna Cossitt). **A Brief View of Cumberland College, Founded by the Synod of the Cumberland Presbyterian Church, Near Princeton, Kentucky. By a Committee of Synod 1828**. Washington, D.C., 1829.

Evans, Henry Bascom. "History of the Organization and Administration of Cumberland Presbyterian Colleges." Ph.D. dissertation, George Peabody College for Teachers, 1938.

Gore, Matthew H. **A History of the Cumberland Presbyterian Church in Kentucky to 1988**. Memphis, Tennessee, 2000.

"Historical Marker Points to Site of Cumberland College at Princeton, Ky." **The Cumberland Presbyterian**, 144 (November 21, 1972), 8.

Howard, J. M., and J. M. Hubbert. "The Cumberland Presbyterian Church." **Presbyterians: A Popular Narrative of their Origin, Progress, Doctrines, and Achievements**. New York, 1892.

Irby, Joe Ben. **Life and Thought of Milton Bird, DD: An Apologist for Cumberland Presbyterian Theology**. Memphis, Tennessee, 2002.

McDonnold, B. W. **History of the Cumberland Presbyterian Church**. Nashville, Tennessee, 1899.

McLean, Finis E. "Cumberland College." **The Union Evangelist**, I (March 11, 1841), 1.

Minutes of Cumberland Synod of the Cumberland Presbyterian Church, 1825-1828. Historical Foundation and Archives of the Cumberland Presbyterian Church and the Cumberland Presbyterian Church in America, Memphis, Tennessee.

Minutes of Logan Presbytery of the Cumberland Presbyterian Church, 1825-1826. Historical Foundation and Archives of the Cumberland Presbyterian Church and the Cumberland Presbyterian Church in America, Memphis, Tennessee.

Minutes of the General Assembly of the Cumberland Presbyterian Church, 1829-1861. Historical Foundation and Archives of the Cumberland Presbyterian Church and the Cumberland Presbyterian Church in America, Memphis, Tennessee.

Smith, M. M., "The First Decade of Cumberland College." **The Cumberland Presbyterian** (February 1, 1900), 139.

Street, Thomas P. "Cumberland College in 1829." **Register of the Kentucky Historical Society**, 66 (October 1968), 392-399.

"Thomas Church Brownell," Virtual American Biographies. Retrieved February 11, 2007, from http://famousamericans.net/.

"Treasurer's Book of Cumberland College, 1826-1848." Alphabetic typescript by Sam Steger. Princeton, Kentucky, Public Library.

Unless stated otherwise, sources can be found in the collection of the Historical Foundation of the Cumberland Presbyterian Church and the Cumberland Presbyterian Church in America, 8207 Traditional Place, Cordova, Tennessee, 38016-7414.

Index

111

112

114

115

116

118

119

120

www.ingramcontent.com/pod-product-compliance
Lightning Source LLC
Chambersburg PA
CBHW021405090426
42742CB00009B/1020